The Complete 50 Lost Book Apocrypha

History of non canonical Bible, The Ethiopian Bible, the lost book of Eden, The book of Enoch, Jasher and Jubilees with the Deuterocanon and Pseudepigrapha

BY

Lebanon Paul

The Complete 50 Lost Book Apocrypha

The Complete 50 Lost Book Apocrypha

TABLE OF CONTENTS

The Complete 50 Lost Book Apocrypha

PART I: Introduction and

Historical Context

Chapter One

Genesis of the Lost Books

In the vast tapestry of biblical narratives, there exists a collection of writings often shrouded in mystery—the lost books that weave a unique thread through the fabric of religious history. Unveiling the mystery behind these texts opens a portal to an intricate world of ancient wisdom, spiritual insights, and narratives that have, for various reasons, been excluded from the standard canon of the Bible. This chapter delves into the genesis of these lost books, seeking to illuminate the reasons behind their exclusion and exploring the historical significance that underpins their existence.

Unveiling the Mystery

The mystery surrounding the lost books stems from their exclusion from the widely accepted canon of the Bible. These texts, including the Book of Enoch, Jasher, Jubilees, and the lost Book of Eden, present unique perspectives on creation, divine interactions, and the human experience. Unveiling this mystery requires a careful examination of the criteria used to determine the canonical status of biblical texts. Issues of authorship, doctrinal alignment, and ecclesiastical acceptance come to the forefront.

One of the contributing factors to the mystery is the varying opinions and criteria employed by different religious traditions. The Ethiopian Orthodox Tewahedo Church, for instance, has embraced certain books that are considered apocryphal by other Christian denominations. As we unravel the mystery, it becomes evident that the exclusion or inclusion of these texts is not solely based on a universally agreed-upon set of criteria but rather reflects the diverse theological perspectives and historical contexts within which different religious communities emerged.

Historical Significance

The historical significance of the lost books cannot be overstated. These writings offer a window into the cultural and religious milieu of ancient societies, providing valuable insights into the beliefs, practices, and worldview of the people who composed and preserved these texts. For example, the Book of Enoch, attributed to the biblical figure Enoch, offers a glimpse into the apocalyptic thinking prevalent in certain Jewish circles during the Second Temple period. It introduces readers to a cosmic journey and detailed visions that influenced later apocalyptic literature.

Jasher and Jubilees contribute historical and chronological dimensions to biblical narratives, providing additional details about events and characters mentioned in the canonical scriptures. The lost Book of Eden, often alluded to but absent from standard Bibles, adds layers to the story of creation and the human condition. Understanding the historical context of these writings enriches our appreciation of the biblical narrative and sheds light on the diverse expressions of faith within ancient communities.

The Ethiopian Bible's Role

Central to the understanding of the lost books is the role played by the Ethiopian Bible in preserving and valuing these texts. The Ethiopian Orthodox Tewahedo Church, with a heritage dating back to the early centuries of Christianity, has maintained a canon that includes several books not found in most Western Bibles. The Ethiopian Bible, also known as the Ge'ez Bible, stands as a testament to the diversity of biblical traditions.

The Ethiopian canon encompasses the complete 81-book Bible, incorporating the lost books and the Deuterocanon, which are absent from many Protestant and some Eastern Orthodox canons. This inclusion highlights the unique theological perspectives of the Ethiopian Orthodox Church and its commitment to preserving a broader range of sacred texts. Understanding the Ethiopian Bible's role in safeguarding these writings provides a lens through which we can appreciate the rich tapestry of biblical traditions and the dynamic nature of the biblical canon across different Christian communities.

In summary, the genesis of the lost books is a tale of mystery, historical significance, and diverse religious traditions. Unveiling this mystery requires an exploration of the criteria for canonical inclusion, while recognizing the historical significance of these texts adds depth to our understanding of ancient beliefs. The Ethiopian Bible, with its distinctive canon, serves as a guardian of these lost books, inviting us to embrace the diversity within the biblical narrative. As we embark on this journey, we peel back the layers of time, seeking to comprehend the intricate interplay between faith, history, and the sacred texts that have shaped the spiritual landscape.

Chapter Two

Understanding the Apocrypha

Definition and Scope

To embark on a journey of understanding the Apocrypha is to navigate through a landscape of sacred writings that, though not universally recognized as part of the canonical Bible, hold profound significance for many. The term "Apocrypha" itself evokes both curiosity and controversy. Defined as a collection of religious texts outside the canonical scriptures, the Apocrypha encompasses a diverse range of writings, including historical narratives, wisdom literature, and apocalyptic visions. These texts often bridge the gap between the Old and New Testaments, offering insights into the religious and cultural milieu of the times.

The scope of the Apocrypha extends beyond the familiar boundaries of the Protestant and Hebrew Bibles. While some Christian denominations, particularly those of the Western traditions, consider these books as deuterocanonical or even apocryphal, others, like the Eastern Orthodox and Ethiopian Orthodox Churches, incorporate them into their canonical scriptures. This diversity in acceptance reflects the complex tapestry of Christian traditions and the varied perspectives on which books are deemed divinely inspired.

Exploring the Apocrypha requires a nuanced understanding of its multifaceted nature. The collection includes books such as Tobit, Judith, Wisdom of Solomon, Sirach (Ecclesiasticus), and additions to canonical books like Daniel and Esther. Each text bears unique cultural, historical, and theological characteristics, contributing to the richness of the Christian narrative. The Apocrypha, thus, stands as a testament to the diversity of voices within the broader biblical tradition, offering a reservoir of wisdom and inspiration for those willing to delve into its pages.

Canonical Controversies

At the heart of understanding the Apocrypha lies the intricate web of canonical controversies that has surrounded these writings for centuries. The debates over which books should be included in the official biblical canon have fueled theological discussions, ecclesiastical disputes, and divergent interpretations within the Christian faith. The Apocrypha, often viewed as a contested territory, has been subject to varying degrees of acceptance and rejection throughout history.

One of the primary canonical controversies surrounding the Apocrypha is its exclusion from the Protestant Bible. The Protestant Reformation in the 16th century witnessed a deliberate decision to exclude certain books, known as the Deuterocanon, from the Protestant canon. This decision, influenced by theological and doctrinal considerations, further accentuated the divide between Protestant and Catholic traditions, as the latter continued to embrace these books.

In contrast, the Eastern Orthodox Churches, including the Ethiopian Orthodox Tewahedo Church, have maintained a broader canon that includes the Apocrypha. The Ethiopian Bible, recognized for its unique collection of 81 books, stands as a living testimony to the acceptance of these writings within certain Christian traditions. The canonical controversies surrounding the Apocrypha, therefore, underscore the dynamic nature of the biblical canon and the ongoing dialogue within the Christian community regarding the scope of divine revelation.

The rejection or acceptance of the Apocrypha is not merely a historical footnote but continues to shape the theological landscape of Christianity today. The controversies surrounding its canonicity prompt believers to wrestle with questions of inspiration, authority, and the discernment of divine revelation. As Christians grapple with these canonical controversies, they are invited to explore the depths of their faith, engaging in a thoughtful examination of the texts that have both challenged and enriched the spiritual journey throughout centuries.

Theological Perspectives

Understanding the Apocrypha necessitates a nuanced exploration of the theological perspectives that underpin these ancient texts. The theological dimensions of the Apocrypha are multifaceted, ranging from reflections on God's providence and wisdom to ethical teachings and apocalyptic visions. These writings contribute to the broader theological discourse within Christianity, offering distinctive insights that complement the canonical scriptures.

One theological thread woven throughout the Apocrypha is the emphasis on divine wisdom. Books like Wisdom of Solomon and Sirach delve into the nature of wisdom, portraying it as a guiding force in the moral and ethical dimensions of human life. The personification of wisdom as a divine attribute aligns with the biblical understanding of God as the source of all wisdom, inviting readers to contemplate the profound relationship between divine insight and human conduct.

Ethical teachings within the Apocrypha provide practical guidance for righteous living. Tobit, for example, emphasizes the importance of almsgiving, prayer, and obedience to God's commandments. Judith, through her courageous actions, becomes a symbol of faith and resilience. These ethical dimensions enrich the theological tapestry of the Apocrypha, underscoring the interconnectedness of belief and practice in the Christian life.

Apocalyptic visions, a prominent theme in certain Apocryphal books, offer glimpses into cosmic realities and divine judgments. The Book of Enoch, though not universally accepted, presents apocalyptic visions attributed to the biblical figure Enoch. These visions, characterized by symbolic imagery and cosmic events, contribute to the broader apocalyptic tradition within Judaism and Christianity, shaping eschatological expectations.

Exploring the Apocrypha from a theological perspective requires an acknowledgment of its diverse theological expressions. While some books emphasize wisdom and ethical teachings, others delve into historical narratives or apocalyptic visions. The theological perspectives within the Apocrypha contribute to the mosaic of Christian beliefs, fostering a deeper understanding of God's nature, human existence, and the intricate interplay between the two.

Therefore, understanding the Apocrypha unveils a rich tapestry of diverse writings that have shaped the Christian tradition. The definition and scope of the Apocrypha encompass a wide array of texts, each offering unique insights into the religious and cultural contexts of their composition. Canonical controversies surrounding these writings have fueled theological discussions and continue to influence the contours of the biblical canon within different Christian traditions. Exploring the theological perspectives within the Apocrypha reveals a multifaceted discourse on divine wisdom, ethical teachings, and apocalyptic visions, enriching the theological tapestry of Christianity. As believers engage with these ancient texts, they embark on a journey that transcends denominational boundaries, inviting them to discover the enduring relevance of the Apocrypha in their spiritual pilgrimage.

Chapter Three

The Lost Book of Eden

Rediscovery and Authenticity

The Lost Book of Eden stands as an enigmatic treasure, a fragment of the sacred narrative that tantalizes the imagination and beckons seekers of ancient wisdom. The rediscovery of this elusive text unveils a journey through time, tracing the footsteps of those who safeguarded, lost, and ultimately recovered it. The authenticity of the Lost Book of Eden, often questioned and debated, requires a meticulous examination of historical clues, linguistic analysis, and theological coherence.

Rediscovering the Lost Book of Eden is akin to a pilgrimage through the annals of history. The allure of Eden, the biblical paradise lost, has captivated minds for centuries. In the 19th century, the quest to reclaim fragments of this lost narrative gained momentum with the discovery of ancient manuscripts. The recovery of texts like the Gospel of Mary, the Apocalypse of Peter, and fragments of the Book of Enoch heightened the anticipation of unearthing the elusive Lost Book of Eden.

The pivotal moment in this quest occurred with the discovery of the Nag Hammadi Library in 1945, buried in the Egyptian desert. Among the codices found, the Gospel of Thomas and the Gospel of Philip were recovered, shedding light on early Christian thought.

While the Lost Book of Eden itself was not among the Nag Hammadi discoveries, the unearthing of these Gnostic texts revitalized scholarly interest in uncovering lost or suppressed Christian writings.

The authenticity of the Lost Book of Eden is a subject of scholarly scrutiny and theological debate. The criteria for determining authenticity involve linguistic analysis, historical context, and theological coherence with established Christian beliefs. Scholars engage in a delicate dance with the past, carefully examining the language and script of discovered manuscripts to discern whether they align with the cultural and linguistic characteristics of the ancient world. This meticulous examination is essential in establishing the provenance and authenticity of the Lost Book of Eden, guiding believers and scholars alike in navigating the blurred boundaries of rediscovery.

Content Overview

The journey into the Lost Book of Eden reveals a narrative that intertwines with the familiar Genesis account, offering a nuanced and expanded perspective on the creation narrative, Adam and Eve, and their subsequent experiences. As readers delve into the content, they encounter vivid imagery and detailed storytelling that unveils layers of theological reflection and spiritual insight.

The Lost Book of Eden begins with an alternative account of the creation of Adam and Eve, introducing celestial beings and divine wisdom in the process. It delves into the intricacies of the Garden of Eden, portraying it not merely as a physical location but as a metaphysical realm where spiritual truths intersect with the material world. The narrative provides detailed conversations between Adam, Eve, and celestial beings, unraveling the complexities of their relationships and the implications of their choices.

The narrative thread extends beyond the expulsion from Eden, exploring the challenges faced by Adam and Eve in the aftermath of their disobedience. The Lost Book of Eden delves into the consequences of their actions, both earthly and spiritual, shedding light on the cosmic dimensions of their choices. The story unfolds with a richness of detail, presenting dialogues, visions, and encounters that expand the biblical narrative, inviting readers to reconsider familiar stories with fresh eyes.

The content of the Lost Book of Eden also delves into the concept of divine knowledge and the pursuit of wisdom. Celestial beings impart insights and revelations to Adam and Eve, offering a glimpse into the mysteries of the spiritual realm. Themes of cosmic knowledge, divine wisdom, and the intertwining of the heavenly and earthly realms permeate the narrative, contributing to a broader understanding of the theological underpinnings within the Lost Book of Eden.

Theological Themes

Exploring the theological themes within the Lost Book of Eden unveils a tapestry of reflections on creation, human nature, and the divine-human relationship. The alternative account of creation presented in this lost text invites believers to reflect on the theological implications of celestial beings, divine wisdom, and the interplay between the spiritual and material realms.

One of the prominent theological themes in the Lost Book of Eden is the concept of divine wisdom. The celestial beings, often portrayed as messengers of divine wisdom, play a central role in guiding Adam and Eve through their spiritual journey. This emphasis on wisdom aligns with the broader biblical tradition, where wisdom is personified as a divine attribute. The Lost Book of Eden expands on this theme, exploring the transformative power of divine knowledge and the implications of seeking wisdom in both earthly and spiritual contexts.

The narrative also grapples with the consequences of human disobedience and the complexity of divine justice. As Adam and Eve navigate the aftermath of their choices, the theological reflections within the Lost Book of Eden delve into questions of sin, redemption, and the nature of God's mercy. The interactions between celestial beings and the human protagonists illuminate the delicate balance between judgment and compassion, inviting readers to ponder the theological implications of divine justice.

Furthermore, the Lost Book of Eden contributes to the theological discourse on the nature of humanity. The alternative account of creation and the nuanced portrayal of Adam and Eve offer insights into the complexity of human nature, encompassing both earthly and spiritual dimensions. This theological exploration challenges traditional understandings of human existence, encouraging believers to engage with the theological complexities embedded within the narrative.

Chapter Four

The Book of Enoch Unveiled

Enoch's Prophetic Vision

The Book of Enoch, an ancient and enigmatic text, unfolds a narrative that transcends the conventional boundaries of biblical storytelling. At the heart of this revelation is Enoch, a figure of antiquity, whose prophetic vision offers a glimpse into celestial realms, divine mysteries, and the unfolding tapestry of cosmic history. Enoch's journey, captured within the pages of this apocalyptic work, unveils a visionary experience that transcends the ordinary boundaries of human understanding.

Enoch, a descendant of Adam, emerges as a central figure in the Book of Enoch, offering a unique perspective on the divine. The narrative begins with Enoch's extraordinary encounters with celestial beings, a journey that transcends the earthly realm and delves into the mysteries of the heavens. Enoch's prophetic vision unfolds against the backdrop of angelic revelations and cosmic landscapes, presenting a vivid tapestry of divine communication that challenges the boundaries of human perception.

The Book of Enoch details Enoch's visionary experiences, encompassing journeys through heavenly realms, encounters with angelic beings, and revelations about the nature of creation and the divine plan. Enoch's prophetic vision goes beyond the temporal constraints of human existence, providing glimpses into the eternal and cosmic dimensions of reality. The narrative intricately weaves together celestial landscapes, symbolic imagery, and profound insights, inviting readers to accompany Enoch on a spiritual pilgrimage that transcends the ordinary bounds of human experience.

As Enoch navigates through the celestial spheres, the Book of Enoch presents a cosmic worldview that enriches the tapestry of biblical thought. The prophetic vision of Enoch encompasses not only the immediate future but extends into eschatological realities, offering a panoramic view of divine intentions and the unfolding of history. This prophetic dimension of Enoch's journey within the Book of Enoch stands as a testament to the visionary nature of biblical revelation, where human intermediaries, like Enoch, become vessels for divine communication that transcends the limits of earthly understanding.

Angelic Revelations

Central to the Book of Enoch are the angelic revelations that Enoch encounters during his visionary journey. The narrative introduces readers to a diverse array of celestial beings, each with specific roles, responsibilities, and insights into the cosmic order. These angels, often referred to as Watchers and holy ones, unveil celestial secrets, divine judgments, and the intricacies of the spiritual realms.

The Watchers, a group of angels mentioned in the Book of Enoch, play a pivotal role in the unfolding narrative. They are depicted as beings who, against divine orders, descend to Earth, interact with humanity, and share forbidden knowledge. The angelic revelations within the Book of Enoch thus introduce a complex interplay between celestial beings and the human experience. The forbidden knowledge imparted by the Watchers becomes a focal point, raising questions about the consequences of human access to divine secrets.

The Book of Enoch provides detailed accounts of angelic interactions, including the naming of specific angels, their hierarchical order, and the cosmic events that unfold as a result of their actions. This intricate portrayal of angelic beings contributes to a broader understanding of the heavenly realms and the role of celestial entities in shaping human destiny. The angelic revelations within the Book of Enoch, though unconventional in the canonical biblical tradition, offer a unique lens through which readers can explore the mysteries of the divine and the intricate relationships between the heavenly and earthly realms.

The angelic revelations also delve into eschatological themes, unveiling insights into the cosmic events that will transpire at the end of times. The Book of Enoch presents a vision of judgment, resurrection, and the establishment of divine justice. The angelic revelations become a source of both illumination and warning, inviting readers to contemplate the consequences of human choices and the ultimate unfolding of God's plan for creation.

Impact on Judeo-Christian Thought

The Book of Enoch's influence on Judeo-Christian thought is profound and far-reaching, shaping theological perspectives, apocalyptic traditions, and the understanding of angelic beings within the broader biblical context. Though not included in the canonical Scriptures of most major religious traditions, the Book of Enoch has left an indelible mark on the religious imagination, contributing to a rich tapestry of beliefs and interpretations.

Enoch's prophetic vision and the angelic revelations within the Book of Enoch have influenced eschatological expectations within Judeo-Christian thought. The detailed accounts of cosmic events, divine judgments, and the ultimate establishment of God's reign have resonated with apocalyptic traditions, impacting how believers envision the culmination of human history. The Book of Enoch, with its vivid portrayal of the end times, has become a source of inspiration for apocalyptic literature and theological reflections on the future.

The understanding of angelic beings within Judeo-Christian thought has also been influenced by the Book of Enoch. The depiction of angels as celestial entities with distinct roles and responsibilities has contributed to a nuanced understanding of the spiritual realms. While the canonical Scriptures mention angels, the Book of Enoch provides additional details about the hierarchy, functions, and interactions of these celestial beings. This influence extends to artistic representations, theological discourse, and cultural expressions that draw upon the rich imagery presented in the Book of Enoch.

Moreover, the impact of the Book of Enoch on Judeo-Christian thought is evident in the reception and usage of its themes and motifs within later religious texts. References to Enoch and the angelic revelations can be found in various Jewish and Christian writings, demonstrating the enduring influence of this apocalyptic work. The Book of Enoch's impact extends beyond doctrinal considerations to shape the broader religious consciousness, inspiring believers to contemplate the mysteries of the divine, the complexities of angelic realms, and the cosmic dimensions of human existence.

The Complete 50 Lost Book Apocrypha

Chapter Five

Jasher and Jubilees - Forgotten Narratives

Comparative Analysis

Jasher and Jubilees, though often relegated to the shadows of biblical literature, emerge as compelling voices that echo through the corridors of forgotten narratives. A comparative analysis of these ancient texts unravels a tapestry of forgotten wisdom, historical accounts, and theological reflections that challenge the conventional boundaries of biblical storytelling. While Jasher and Jubilees share certain similarities, they each possess a distinct flavor, contributing unique threads to the fabric of biblical literature.

In the comparative analysis, Jasher stands out as a historical narrative that supplements and expands upon events found in the canonical books of Genesis and Joshua. The title "Jasher," meaning the upright or righteous one, implies a commitment to preserving historical accuracy and righteousness. The Book of Jasher, mentioned in Joshua 10:13 and 2 Samuel 1:18, is not part of the standard biblical canon, yet it finds a place in the cultural memory of biblical traditions. Its contents include additional details about the lives of biblical figures such as Adam, Noah, Abraham, and Moses, presenting a chronological account that complements the canonical narratives.

Jubilees, on the other hand, bears a different character as it weaves a tapestry of biblical history through a calendrical lens. Also known as the Book of Jubilees or the Little Genesis, this text organizes events according to a jubilee cycle, offering a unique perspective on the divine plan. Jubilees presents itself as a revelation to Moses on Mount Sinai, providing insights into the biblical narratives from the creation of the world to the giving of the law. The calendrical structure of Jubilees, dividing time into sets of 49 years, adds a distinctive layer to its comparative analysis with Jasher, emphasizing the ordered progression of divine history.

While both Jasher and Jubilees share a penchant for expanding upon biblical narratives, their comparative analysis reveals nuanced differences in style, content, and thematic emphasis. Jasher leans towards historical detail, offering a richer context to familiar stories, while Jubilees adopts a chronological framework that emphasizes the divine plan and the sanctification of time.

Thematic Threads

Exploring the thematic threads within Jasher and Jubilees unveils a tapestry of interconnected narratives that enrich the biblical landscape. Jasher, in its thematic exploration, focuses on righteousness as a guiding principle throughout history. The very title of the book suggests an emphasis on uprightness, moral conduct, and fidelity to divine principles. As Jasher unfolds, readers encounter not only historical accounts but also reflections on the righteous choices made by biblical figures in the face of moral dilemmas.

The thematic threads of Jasher intertwine with the biblical narrative, presenting a parallel account that highlights the moral character of key figures. The righteous deeds of individuals like Noah, Abraham, and Moses become central to the narrative, emphasizing the significance of moral integrity in the unfolding divine plan. Jasher, through its thematic emphasis on righteousness, invites readers to reflect on the ethical dimensions of human choices and the enduring impact of righteousness on the course of history.

In Jubilees, the thematic threads are woven into the fabric of a divinely ordered time structure. The concept of jubilees, each spanning 49 years, becomes a key thematic element, signifying not only the passage of time but also the cycles of divine blessings and judgments. The calendrical emphasis in Jubilees contributes to its thematic exploration of divine order, emphasizing the meticulous planning of God throughout history. Each jubilee marks a significant event in the divine plan, from creation to the giving of the law, creating a rhythmic pattern that underscores the sanctification of time.

The thematic threads within Jubilees extend beyond chronology to encompass divine revelation, covenantal fidelity, and the role of angels in human affairs. The angelic interactions presented in Jubilees provide additional layers to the thematic exploration, introducing celestial beings who play distinct roles in the unfolding divine drama. The book's thematic emphasis on divine order, revelation, and angelic interventions invites readers to contemplate the intricacies of the divine plan and the interconnectedness of human and celestial realms.

Their Place in Biblical Literature

Jasher and Jubilees, though not included in the standard biblical canon, hold a unique place in biblical literature, offering supplementary perspectives that echo through the corridors of tradition. The omission of these texts from the canonical Scriptures does not diminish their significance within certain Jewish and Christian communities, where they are regarded as valuable reservoirs of historical and theological insights.

Jasher, with its thematic emphasis on righteousness and historical expansion, serves as a companion to the canonical books of Genesis and Joshua. Its recounting of familiar stories with additional details contributes to a broader understanding of the moral dimensions of biblical figures and the unfolding divine plan. While not universally recognized as authoritative, Jasher finds resonance within cultural memory, influencing interpretations and reflections on the lives of key biblical characters.

Jubilees, with its calendrical framework and thematic exploration of divine order, occupies a distinctive place in biblical literature. The book's organization of events according to jubilees provides a unique lens through which readers can engage with the biblical narrative.

Despite not achieving canonical status in most traditions, Jubilees has left an indelible mark on certain theological reflections, especially those concerned with divine planning, covenantal history, and the sanctification of time.

The place of Jasher and Jubilees in biblical literature extends beyond their absence from the canonical Scriptures. These texts function as witnesses to diverse interpretive traditions, cultural expressions, and theological reflections within Judaism and Christianity. The fact that these texts were preserved and transmitted, even if not universally accepted, underscores their enduring relevance within certain religious communities.

PART II: The Ethiopian Bible

and Its Unique Canon

Chapter Six

The Ethiopian Orthodox Tewahedo Church

Historical Roots

The Ethiopian Orthodox Tewahedo Church, with its deep historical roots, stands as a venerable institution that has preserved a distinctive expression of Christianity for centuries. The origins of Christianity in Ethiopia are intertwined with biblical narratives, tradition, and the ancient Aksumite Empire. According to Ethiopian tradition, the introduction of Christianity to the region is attributed to the encounter between the Ethiopian eunuch and the Apostle Philip, as narrated in the Book of Acts (Acts 8:26-39). This encounter is considered a pivotal moment in Ethiopian Christian history, marking the foundation of a faith that would become integral to the identity of the Ethiopian people.

The historical roots of the Ethiopian Orthodox Tewahedo Church further extend to the fourth century when Christianity was declared the state religion of the Aksumite Empire under King Ezana. This early adoption of Christianity distinguishes Ethiopia as one of the first nations to officially embrace the Christian faith. The connection between the Aksumite rulers and the Holy Land, symbolized by the legendary Ark of the Covenant housed in Aksum, contributed to the church's historical significance and its identity as a guardian of sacred traditions.

Throughout the centuries, the Ethiopian Orthodox Tewahedo Church has weathered political upheavals, foreign invasions, and cultural transformations. The church's resilience is a testament to its enduring historical roots and its ability to adapt while preserving a unique expression of Christianity deeply rooted in ancient traditions. The Ethiopian church's historical journey reflects not only the growth of Christianity in the region but also its integration into the cultural, social, and political fabric of Ethiopia.

Canonical Distinctions

Central to the identity of the Ethiopian Orthodox Tewahedo Church are its canonical distinctions, which include a broader canon of scripture than that recognized by many Western Christian denominations. The Ethiopian Bible, known as the Ge'ez Bible, encompasses the standard 66 books found in most Protestant Bibles, along with additional books known as the "Narrower Canon." This narrower canon includes several books labeled as deuterocanonical or apocryphal by other traditions, such as the Book of Enoch, Jubilees, Jasher, and additional Psalms.

The canonical distinctions of the Ethiopian Orthodox Tewahedo Church extend beyond the inclusion of apocryphal books. The church recognizes the

64

Deuterocanon, which consists of books like Tobit, Judith, Wisdom of Solomon, Sirach (Ecclesiasticus), Baruch, and the additions to Daniel and Esther. These books, while present in the Ethiopian canon, are often excluded from the canons of many Protestant Bibles.

The Ethiopian church's canonical distinctions are deeply rooted in its historical development and theological traditions. The acceptance of a broader canon reflects the church's commitment to preserving ancient sacred texts that hold cultural and spiritual significance for its members. The canonical distinctions of the Ethiopian Orthodox Tewahedo Church, though divergent from certain Western traditions, underline the dynamic nature of the biblical canon within the broader Christian tapestry.

Cultural Significance

Beyond its religious functions, the Ethiopian Orthodox Tewahedo Church holds immense cultural significance as a focal point for Ethiopian identity and heritage. The church has played a central role in shaping the cultural landscape of Ethiopia, influencing art, music, literature, and societal norms. The intertwining of Christian traditions with indigenous Ethiopian culture has resulted in a unique synthesis that permeates various aspects of daily life.

The celebration of religious festivals, such as Timket (Epiphany) and Meskel (Finding of the True Cross), involves vibrant processions, colorful rituals, and communal celebrations. These events not only hold religious significance but also serve as expressions of cultural pride and identity. The distinctive Ethiopian style of religious art and iconography, characterized by intricate paintings, murals, and illuminated manuscripts, further exemplifies the fusion of religious devotion and cultural expression within the Ethiopian Orthodox Tewahedo Church.

The church's cultural significance is also evident in its influence on Ethiopian literature. The Ge'ez language, used in liturgical texts, biblical translations, and religious literature, has shaped the development of written Ethiopian languages. The creation of religious manuscripts, some of which contain apocryphal books unique to the Ethiopian canon, reflects the artistic and cultural contributions of the church to Ethiopia's literary heritage.

Furthermore, the Ethiopian Orthodox Tewahedo Church has been a custodian of sacred artifacts, including ancient crosses, manuscripts, and religious relics. The Ark of the Covenant, believed by Ethiopian tradition to be housed in the Church of St. Mary of Zion in Aksum, holds particular cultural and religious significance. Pilgrimages to this church and other religious sites contribute to a sense of shared cultural identity and spiritual pilgrimage among Ethiopian Christians.

Chapter Seven

Exploring the Ethiopian Bible

Canonical Structure

The Ethiopian Bible, known as the Ge'ez Bible, stands as a remarkable compilation of sacred texts that reflects the spiritual heritage of the Ethiopian Orthodox Tewahedo Church. Its canonical structure distinguishes it from other Christian traditions, embodying a unique tapestry of sacred literature that extends beyond the standard canon. The Ethiopian Bible shares the foundational 66 books found in many Christian Bibles, but it encompasses additional writings that constitute the

"Narrower Canon" or "Broader Canon," depending on denominational perspectives.

The canonical structure of the Ethiopian Bible follows the divisions familiar to many Christians: the Old Testament and the New Testament. However, within these overarching divisions, the Ethiopian canon unfolds with distinctive features. The Old Testament, known as the "Octateuch," comprises the standard books found in most Christian Bibles, including Genesis, Exodus, Leviticus, Numbers, Deuteronomy, Joshua, Judges, and Ruth. Beyond this Octateuch, the Ethiopian Old Testament includes the "Narrower Canon" or deuterocanonical books such as Tobit, Judith, Wisdom of Solomon, Sirach (Ecclesiasticus), Baruch, and the additions to Daniel and Esther.

The New Testament of the Ethiopian Bible aligns with the standard Christian canon, featuring the Gospels, Acts, Pauline and General Epistles, and the Book of Revelation. However, the Ethiopian New Testament also incorporates the broader canon, with additional books such as the Book of Enoch, Jubilees, Jasher, and 1 and 2 Clement. The inclusion of these apocryphal and pseudepigraphical texts in the Ethiopian canon reflects a distinctive approach to the biblical narrative, encompassing a broader range of sacred writings.

Unique Books and Translations

Within the Ethiopian Bible's expansive canon, certain books stand out as unique contributions to the rich tapestry of sacred literature. The inclusion of books like the Book of Enoch, Jubilees, and Jasher provides additional layers to the biblical narrative, offering insights into celestial visions, calendrical structures, and historical expansions. These unique books, labeled as apocryphal or pseudepigraphical by some Christian traditions, play a significant role in shaping the theological reflections and spiritual identity of the Ethiopian Orthodox Tewahedo Church.

The Book of Enoch, for example, contributes an apocalyptic perspective that delves into celestial realms, angelic interactions, and eschatological visions. Jubilees introduces a calendrical framework that organizes biblical events within a cyclical pattern, emphasizing the divine order and sanctification of time. Jasher expands upon the historical narratives found in Genesis and

Joshua, offering additional details about key figures and events. These unique books, although not universally recognized in the canonical Scriptures of other Christian denominations, have found a home within the Ethiopian Bible, enriching its narrative with diverse theological themes.

The Ethiopian Bible's unique contributions extend beyond its canon to the translations and linguistic diversity within its sacred texts. The Ge'ez language, an ancient Ethiopian language, serves as the medium for many of the biblical manuscripts. Translations of the Bible into Ge'ez have played a crucial role in preserving the sacred text and making it accessible to Ethiopian Christians. The process of translation involves not only linguistic considerations but also cultural nuances, ensuring that the sacred message resonates with the hearts and minds of the faithful.

Moreover, the Ethiopian Bible incorporates distinct translations of certain books. For example, the Ethiopian version of the Book of Enoch, also known as 1 Enoch, differs in some aspects from other translations of this apocryphal text. These variations in translation contribute to the unique character of the Ethiopian Bible, reflecting the cultural and linguistic context within which the sacred texts are transmitted and interpreted.

Ritual and Liturgical Uses

The Ethiopian Bible transcends its role as a sacred text and becomes a focal point for rituals and liturgical practices within the Ethiopian Orthodox Tewahedo

Church. The ritual and liturgical uses of the Ethiopian Bible underscore its central position in the worship and spiritual life of the Ethiopian Christian community. The sacred text becomes more than a repository of theological truths; it becomes a dynamic tool for communal worship, spiritual formation, and the transmission of sacred traditions.

One of the prominent liturgical uses of the Ethiopian Bible is in the celebration of the Divine Liturgy. The Scriptures, including readings from both the Old and New Testaments, are integral to the liturgical structure. The Ethiopian Orthodox Tewahedo Church follows a liturgical calendar that includes various feasts, fasts, and commemorations, each accompanied by specific biblical readings. The readings not only convey the sacred narrative but also guide the faithful through the liturgical seasons, creating a rhythm of worship that aligns with the biblical narrative.

The Ethiopian Bible also plays a crucial role in the sacramental life of the church. The administration of sacraments, such as baptism, confirmation, and the Holy Eucharist, involves scriptural readings that draw from the Ethiopian canon. The use of specific biblical passages during sacramental rituals reinforces the connection between the sacred text and the transformative experiences of the faithful.

Beyond formal liturgical settings, the Ethiopian Bible is woven into the fabric of individual and communal devotional practices. Personal reading of the Scriptures, memorization of key passages, and recitation of prayers based on biblical themes are common aspects of Ethiopian Christian spirituality. The Ethiopian Christian community's familiarity with the broader canon, including apocryphal and pseudepigraphical texts, influences the devotional life of believers and shapes their theological perspectives.

Chapter Eight

The Lost Book of Eden in Ethiopian Tradition

Cultural Adaptations

The Lost Book of Eden, within the context of Ethiopian tradition, unveils a captivating narrative that has left an indelible mark on the cultural and religious tapestry of the Ethiopian Orthodox Tewahedo Church. This ancient text, often referred to as the Ethiopian Book of Adam and Eve, recounts the story of the first human couple, Adam and Eve, and their experiences in the Garden of Eden. The Lost Book of Eden in Ethiopian tradition is not merely a static historical account but a living narrative that has undergone cultural adaptations, integrating itself into the collective consciousness of Ethiopian Christianity.

Cultural adaptations of the Lost Book of Eden are evident in various aspects, including linguistic nuances, artistic expressions, and ritual practices. The Ge'ez language, an ancient Ethiopian language, serves as the linguistic medium through which the Ethiopian Book of Adam and Eve is transmitted. The translation and adaptation of this text into Ge'ez contribute to its resonance within the cultural context of Ethiopia, providing a linguistic bridge that connects the ancient narrative with the lived experiences of Ethiopian Christians.

Artistic expressions also play a crucial role in the cultural adaptations of the Lost Book of Eden. Illuminated manuscripts, paintings, and murals depicting scenes from the Ethiopian Book of Adam and Eve adorn churches, monasteries, and religious artifacts. The artistic representations of Adam, Eve, and the serpent within the Ethiopian context reflect a synthesis of biblical imagery and indigenous artistic styles. These visual adaptations serve not only as aesthetic expressions but also as pedagogical tools, conveying the narrative to those who may not engage directly with the written text.

The Lost Book of Eden has become woven into the fabric of Ethiopian cultural identity, influencing storytelling traditions, oral histories, and communal practices. The adaptability of the narrative allows it to take on new meanings within different cultural contexts, fostering a sense of ownership and relevance among Ethiopian Christians. The Lost Book of Eden, through cultural adaptations, becomes a dynamic and living expression of faith that resonates within the hearts and minds of the Ethiopian Christian community.

Influences on Ethiopian Christianity

The Lost Book of Eden exerts profound influences on Ethiopian Christianity, shaping theological perspectives, moral teachings, and the understanding of the human condition. The narrative of Adam and Eve's experiences in the Garden of Eden offers a unique lens through which Ethiopian Christians contemplate themes of creation, disobedience, redemption, and the consequences of sin. The influences of the Lost Book of Eden extend beyond doctrinal considerations to permeate ethical reflections, spiritual disciplines, and the lived experiences of believers.

The Ethiopian interpretation of the narrative emphasizes the consequences of disobedience and the subsequent redemptive actions of God. The narrative becomes a cautionary tale, underscoring the importance of moral conduct, fidelity to divine commandments, and the recognition of human vulnerability to temptation. Ethiopian Christians, through the influences of the Lost Book of Eden, engage in theological reflections that address the complexities of human nature and the transformative power of divine grace.

Moreover, the Lost Book of Eden contributes to Ethiopian Christianity's understanding of the interconnectedness between the human and divine realms. The narrative unfolds a cosmic drama where celestial beings, such as angels and the adversary, play active roles in the unfolding of human history. The influences of this narrative are evident in Ethiopian theological discourse, where considerations of angelic interventions, divine judgments, and eschatological expectations enrich the broader Christian narrative.

The Lost Book of Eden's influences on Ethiopian Christianity extend to the liturgical and sacramental practices of the Ethiopian Orthodox Tewahedo Church. The narrative becomes an integral part of the church's annual cycle of feasts and fasts, influencing the scriptural readings, hymns, and prayers associated with specific liturgical seasons. The Lost Book of Eden's narrative, with its emphasis on creation and redemption, becomes a thematic anchor within the liturgical calendar, guiding the spiritual journey of Ethiopian Christians through the rhythms of worship.

Ritual Practices

Ritual practices within the Ethiopian Orthodox Tewahedo Church reflect the embedded presence of the Lost Book of Eden in the religious life of the community. The narrative of Adam and Eve's experiences in the Garden of Eden becomes a focal point for certain ritual practices, influencing sacramental moments, penitential acts, and pilgrimages. These rituals, infused with the narrative's themes, become transformative encounters that shape the spiritual consciousness of Ethiopian Christians.

One notable ritual practice influenced by the Lost Book of Eden is the sacrament of confession and repentance. Ethiopian Christians, acknowledging the narrative's portrayal of human frailty and disobedience, engage in ritual acts of confession to seek divine forgiveness. The narrative becomes a moral compass that guides individuals through the process of repentance, emphasizing the importance of acknowledging one's shortcomings and seeking reconciliation with God.

Pilgrimages to religious sites associated with the Lost Book of Eden's narrative also form an essential ritual practice within Ethiopian Christianity. The Church of St.

Mary of Zion in Aksum, believed to house the legendary Ark of the Covenant, is a significant pilgrimage destination. Pilgrims, inspired by the narrative's connection to sacred relics and historical sites, embark on journeys of spiritual significance, seeking a deeper connection with the biblical narrative and the divine presence.

The Lost Book of Eden's influence on ritual practices extends to the liturgical celebration of certain feasts and fasts within the Ethiopian Orthodox Tewahedo Church. The narrative becomes an integral part of the scriptural readings, hymns, and prayers associated with specific liturgical seasons. The fasting practices observed by Ethiopian Christians, especially during Lent, become a spiritual discipline inspired by the narrative's themes of repentance, self-discipline, and preparation for the celebration of the Resurrection.

In conclusion, the Lost Book of Eden in Ethiopian tradition transcends its status as a historical narrative and becomes a dynamic force that shapes the cultural adaptations, influences, and ritual practices within the Ethiopian Orthodox Tewahedo Church. The narrative's resonance within the cultural context of Ethiopia reflects its adaptability and enduring significance as a source of inspiration, guidance, and spiritual transformation. The Lost Book of Eden, within the narrative landscape of Ethiopian Christianity, continues to unfold its profound influences, inviting believers to engage with the timeless themes of creation, disobedience, redemption, and divine grace.

Chapter Nine

Ethiopian Book of Enoch - A Closer Look

Ethiopic Enoch Manuscripts

The Ethiopian Book of Enoch, also known as 1 Enoch, occupies a significant place within the literary and spiritual heritage of the Ethiopian Orthodox Tewahedo Church. The Ethiopic Enoch manuscripts, written in the ancient Ge'ez language, present a closer look into the complex tapestry of this apocryphal text's transmission, preservation, and its impact on Ethiopian spirituality.

The Ethiopic Enoch manuscripts, discovered primarily in the Ethiopian monastic libraries, provide a unique glimpse into the meticulous efforts of scribes and scholars who preserved this ancient text. The manuscripts exhibit variations in content, arrangement, and annotations, suggesting a dynamic tradition of transmission that allowed for adaptations and interpretations. These manuscripts, often adorned with intricate illuminations and marginal notes, reflect not only the textual transmission of 1 Enoch but also the reverence with which it was held within the Ethiopian Christian community.

The Ethiopic Enoch manuscripts encompass the three major sections of 1 Enoch: the Book of the Watchers (1-36), the Book of Parables or Similitudes (37-71), and the Astronomical Book (72-82). Each section contributes distinct theological perspectives, apocalyptic visions, and ethical teachings. The Ethiopic manuscripts' fidelity to the original Aramaic Enochic literature, combined with linguistic adaptations into Ge'ez, showcases the interplay between the text's Semitic origins and its integration into the Ethiopian linguistic and cultural context.

Enochian Influence on Ethiopian Spirituality

The influence of the Ethiopian Book of Enoch on Ethiopian spirituality extends beyond its role as an ancient text; it has become a source of profound inspiration, theological reflection, and spiritual guidance within the Ethiopian Orthodox Tewahedo Church. The

Enochian narrative, with its apocalyptic visions, celestial journeys, and revelations about the nature of creation, resonates deeply with Ethiopian Christians, shaping their understanding of God's mysteries, the cosmos, and humanity's role within the divine plan.

One key aspect of the Enochian influence on Ethiopian spirituality lies in its contributions to the understanding of angels and celestial beings. The Book of the Watchers, within 1 Enoch, unfolds narratives about fallen angels, their interactions with humans, and the consequences of their transgressions. This thematic exploration of angelic realms, divine judgments, and the cosmic order has left an indelible mark on Ethiopian theological perspectives. The Ethiopian Orthodox Tewahedo Church, influenced by Enochian insights, acknowledges the dynamic interactions between the celestial and earthly realms, fostering a sense of divine providence and the active participation of angels in God's unfolding plan.

Moreover, the Enochian influence permeates Ethiopian spirituality through its apocalyptic visions and eschatological themes. The Book of Parables, also known as the Similitudes, unfolds visions of the final judgment, the fate of the righteous and the wicked, and the establishment of God's eternal kingdom. Ethiopian Christians, guided by the Enochian lens, engage in theological reflections about the eschaton, emphasizing themes of righteousness, judgment, and the hope of a renewed creation. The Enochian influence thus becomes a catalyst for a robust eschatological consciousness within the Ethiopian Christian community.

Ethiopian spirituality, enriched by the Enochian narrative, also finds expressions in liturgical practices, devotional life, and the artistic representations of Enochic themes. The Ethiopian Orthodox Tewahedo Church incorporates readings from 1 Enoch into certain liturgical seasons, aligning the Enochian narrative with the church's annual cycle of feasts and fasts. Devotional practices, including prayers and hymns inspired by Enochic themes, become integral components of Ethiopian Christian worship. The artistic representations of Enochic visions, whether in illuminated manuscripts or church murals, serve as visual reminders of the transcendent dimensions of Ethiopian spirituality influenced by the Book of Enoch.

Scholarly Perspectives

Scholarly perspectives on the Ethiopian Book of Enoch shed light on the intricate textual history, theological nuances, and cultural adaptations of this ancient apocryphal text within the Ethiopian context. Academic studies of the Ethiopic Enoch manuscripts, conducted by scholars and researchers, contribute to a deeper understanding of the transmission, reception, and interpretation of 1 Enoch within Ethiopian Christianity.

The scholarly examination of Ethiopic Enoch manuscripts involves meticulous textual criticism, comparative analyses with other Enochic traditions, and investigations into linguistic variations and adaptations. Researchers explore the relationships between the Ge'ez manuscripts and their potential connections to earlier

Aramaic Enochic texts. The pursuit of manuscript traditions, textual variants, and scribal practices illuminates the dynamic nature of the Enochian tradition within Ethiopian literary and religious circles.

Theological perspectives on the Ethiopian Book of Enoch also form a significant area of scholarly inquiry. Scholars engage in exegetical analyses of Enochian themes, probing into the theological implications of celestial visions, the nature of angels, and eschatological motifs. Comparative studies with other Enochic traditions, such as the Qumran Enochic literature, contribute to a broader understanding of the theological developments and adaptations within the Ethiopian context.

Additionally, scholarly perspectives extend to the cultural and social dimensions of Enochian influence within Ethiopian Christianity. Researchers explore the intersections between Enochic themes and indigenous Ethiopian beliefs, rituals, and cultural expressions. The examination of how the Enochian narrative becomes integrated into Ethiopian cultural memory, storytelling traditions, and popular piety reveals the dynamic interplay between sacred texts and lived experiences.

Chapter Ten

Jasher and Jubilees in Ethiopian Faith

Reception and Integration

Within the rich tapestry of Ethiopian Christian faith, the apocryphal books of Jasher and Jubilees unfold as integral threads, contributing distinct hues to the narrative landscape. The reception and integration of these often-overlooked texts within the Ethiopian Orthodox Tewahedo Church illuminate a nuanced relationship between canonical and apocryphal scriptures. This chapter explores how Jasher and

Jubilees, once relegated to the peripheries, have been embraced and woven into the fabric of Ethiopian faith.

The reception of Jasher and Jubilees within Ethiopian Christianity reflects a deliberate effort to engage with a broader range of sacred texts beyond the traditional canon. Jasher, also known as the Book of Jasher or Sefer HaYashar, presents itself as a historical and ethical guide, supplementing narratives found in the canonical books. Jubilees, on the other hand, offers a reimagined chronology of biblical events, framing them within a liturgical and calendrical context. Ethiopian Christians, appreciating the unique perspectives and insights these texts bring, have integrated them into their theological discourse and devotional practices.

The integration of Jasher and Jubilees within the Ethiopian Orthodox Tewahedo Church extends beyond private study to formal education and theological discussions. Seminaries and monastic schools within the Ethiopian Christian tradition often include these apocryphal texts in their curriculum, fostering a deeper understanding of the broader biblical narrative. Scholars and theologians engage in critical examinations of Jasher and Jubilees, exploring their historical context, theological implications, and their resonance within Ethiopian cultural and spiritual traditions.

Liturgical Applications

Liturgical applications of Jasher and Jubilees within Ethiopian Christianity manifest in the incorporation of readings, prayers, and hymns inspired by these apocryphal texts into the worship practices of the Ethiopian Orthodox Tewahedo Church. Liturgical seasons and feasts provide opportune moments for the faithful to encounter the narratives of Jasher and Jubilees within the context of communal worship. The liturgical applications of these apocryphal books contribute to the rhythmic cadence of worship, enriching the spiritual journey of Ethiopian Christians.

Jasher, with its historical accounts and poetic reflections, often finds its way into liturgical readings during specific feast days. Passages from Jasher that align with the themes of the liturgical season become a source of inspiration, connecting the faithful with the broader narrative of God's redemptive plan. The inclusion of Jasher readings in liturgy underscores the belief that these apocryphal texts carry valuable insights and ethical teachings relevant to the spiritual formation of the community.

Jubilees, with its unique calendrical structure and reimagined chronology, lends itself to liturgical applications that resonate with the cyclical nature of the liturgical calendar. Certain passages from Jubilees, particularly those that highlight the sanctification of time and the covenantal relationships between God and humanity, become focal points during liturgical celebrations. Ethiopian Christians, guided by the liturgical applications of Jubilees, perceive time not merely as a linear progression but as a sacred journey within the divine order.

The liturgical use of Jasher and Jubilees within the Ethiopian Christian tradition contributes to a sense of continuity between the canonical and apocryphal scriptures. The intentional integration of these texts into the liturgical life of the church fosters a holistic engagement with the broader biblical narrative, emphasizing the interconnectedness of various scriptural threads within the worshiping community.

Synthesis with Canonical Books

The synthesis of Jasher and Jubilees with the canonical books of the Bible within Ethiopian faith represents a harmonious blending of diverse voices within the sacred narrative. While maintaining a deep reverence for the canonical scriptures, Ethiopian Christians recognize the complementary nature of these apocryphal texts, viewing them as valuable extensions of the biblical tapestry. This synthesis reflects a dynamic approach to scripture that goes beyond rigid boundaries, inviting believers to explore the full spectrum of divine revelation.

Jasher, with its poetic narratives and supplementary historical details, becomes a companion to the canonical books, offering nuanced perspectives on familiar stories. Ethiopian Christians, in their engagement with Jasher, perceive it as a bridge between the gaps in the canonical accounts, shedding light on lesser-known events and figures. This synthesis allows for a more comprehensive understanding of the biblical narrative, enriching the theological reflections and moral teachings embedded within the scriptures.

Jubilees, with its liturgical and calendrical focus, contributes to a synthesis that transcends mere historical narrative. Ethiopian Christians, attuned to the liturgical rhythm inspired by Jubilees, perceive time as a sacred vessel within which the divine unfolds. The synthesis of Jubilees with the canonical books influences the conceptualization of divine covenant, emphasizing the cyclical nature of God's engagement with humanity. This harmonious blending of canonical and apocryphal voices within Ethiopian spirituality results in a holistic and integrated approach to the sacred narrative.

The synthesis of Jasher and Jubilees with canonical books also extends to the realm of theological discourse. Ethiopian theologians engage in dialogues that draw upon the insights gleaned from these apocryphal texts, exploring theological themes such as covenant, justice, and divine providence. The synthesis invites believers to embrace a broader vision of divine revelation, recognizing the diverse expressions of God's wisdom embedded within both canonical and apocryphal scriptures.

PART III: The Deuterocanon -

Expanding the Biblical Canon

Chapter Eleven

Defining the Deuterocanon

Historical Background

The Deuterocanon, often referred to as the "second canon" or "secondary canon," constitutes a distinctive section within the Christian biblical tradition. This chapter delves into the historical background of the Deuterocanon, unraveling the intricate journey of these books as they navigate the currents of time, tradition, and theological discourse.

The historical roots of the Deuterocanon trace back to the Septuagint, the Greek translation of the Hebrew

Scriptures produced in the Hellenistic period. This translation, crafted by Jewish scholars in Alexandria, Egypt, included additional books that did not find a place in the Hebrew Masoretic Text. The term "Deuterocanon" itself conveys the secondary status of these books in comparison to the protocanonical books widely accepted by both Jewish and Protestant traditions.

The earliest Christian communities, influenced by the Septuagint, embraced the Deuterocanon as part of their sacred scripture. Early Christian writings, such as the Epistle of Barnabas and the Shepherd of Hermas, reflect the use of Deuterocanonical books in theological reflections and moral exhortations. The historical background of the Deuterocanon, therefore, reveals a nuanced relationship between Jewish, Christian, and

Hellenistic contexts, shaping the trajectory of these books within the evolving canon.

As Christianity spread and diversified, different regional traditions emerged, each with its own perspective on the inclusion of the Deuterocanon. The Eastern Orthodox Church, aligning with the Septuagint, fully embraced the Deuterocanon, while the Western Christian traditions, influenced by the Latin Vulgate, exhibited variations in their acceptance of these books. The historical background of the Deuterocanon becomes a narrative of transmission, reception, and divergence, reflecting the complex interplay between cultural, linguistic, and theological factors.

Controversies Surrounding Inclusion

The inclusion of the Deuterocanon within the Christian biblical canon has been a subject of controversy and debate throughout history. The controversies surrounding these books are multifaceted, encompassing issues of linguistic variation, theological content, and divergent traditions within the Christian community.

One of the primary controversies revolves around the linguistic variation between the Hebrew Masoretic Text and the Greek Septuagint. Critics argue that the Deuterocanonical books, having originated in Greek, lack the direct Hebrew originals found for the protocanonical books. This linguistic distinction becomes a point of contention, with some questioning the authenticity and authority of the Deuterocanon based on the absence of Hebrew manuscripts.

The theological content of the Deuterocanon also becomes a source of controversy, as certain doctrines and teachings found in these books differ from those in the protocanonical books. The inclusion of Tobit, Judith, Wisdom of Solomon, Sirach, Baruch, 1 and 2 Maccabees, and additions to Daniel and Esther introduces theological nuances not present in the Hebrew Scriptures. The controversies surrounding theological differences range from the intercessory role of angels to prayers for the dead, challenging theological frameworks that have become normative in other Christian traditions.

Divergent traditions within the Christian community contribute to the controversies surrounding the Deuterocanon. While the Eastern Orthodox Church and the Roman Catholic Church accept the Deuterocanon as an integral part of their biblical canon, Protestant traditions, following the principles of the Reformation, exclude these books from the Old Testament. The controversies surrounding inclusion or exclusion become emblematic of broader theological disagreements, emphasizing the complexity of establishing a universally accepted biblical canon.

Theological Implications

The inclusion of the Deuterocanon in the Christian biblical canon carries profound theological implications that resonate across doctrinal, liturgical, and ethical dimensions. As these books find their place within the sacred scriptures, they contribute unique perspectives and theological insights that enrich the Christian understanding of God, humanity, and the divine-human relationship.

One theological implication of the Deuterocanon lies in its exploration of themes related to wisdom, piety, and moral instruction. Books like Sirach and Wisdom of Solomon offer reflections on the nature of wisdom, the pursuit of virtue, and the consequences of righteous and unrighteous actions. Theological reflections drawn from the Deuterocanon contribute to the ethical discourse within the Christian community, guiding believers in matters of personal conduct, social justice, and the cultivation of virtues.

The Deuterocanon also introduces theological perspectives on divine intervention, intercession, and the afterlife. Tobit, for example, portrays the intercessory role of the archangel Raphael, highlighting the active involvement of celestial beings in human affairs. The theological implications of such depictions extend beyond the narrative context to inform beliefs about angelic mediation and divine providence within the broader Christian tradition.

Liturgical practices within Christian traditions that include the Deuterocanon incorporate readings, prayers, and hymns inspired by these books into the worship life of the church. Theological implications of the Deuterocanon manifest in liturgical expressions that resonate with themes of divine mercy, the communion of saints, and the commemoration of significant events such as the Maccabean revolt. The liturgical integration of the Deuterocanon reflects a theological commitment to a comprehensive engagement with sacred scriptures, recognizing the diverse theological voices within the Christian tradition.

Furthermore, the theological implications of the Deuterocanon extend to the Christian understanding of salvation history. The inclusion of 1 and 2 Maccabees provides historical accounts of the Maccabean revolt and the subsequent rededication of the Temple in Jerusalem. These events, while not found in the protocanonical books, contribute to the narrative of God's faithfulness, deliverance, and the restoration of religious practices.

The theological implications of these historical narratives shape the Christian understanding of God's providential care for His people and the enduring quest for religious freedom.

Chapter Twelve

Wisdom Literature in the Deuterocanon

Sirach and Wisdom of Solomon

The Deuterocanon introduces a captivating dimension to biblical literature through its wisdom books—Sirach and Wisdom of Solomon. These books, often regarded as the crown jewels of the Deuterocanon, navigate the expansive terrain of human experience, offering profound reflections on morality, virtue, divine providence, and the nature of wisdom itself.

Sirach, also known as Ecclesiasticus, presents a collection of ethical teachings and practical advice attributed to Jesus Ben Sira, a sage in ancient Jerusalem. This work, written in Hebrew and later translated into Greek, provides a comprehensive guide to righteous living, familial relationships, and societal conduct. Sirach, with its aphoristic style and pragmatic wisdom, becomes a reservoir of insights that illuminate the intricacies of human existence.

Wisdom of Solomon emerges as a philosophical and theological discourse, exploring the nature of wisdom and its interplay with divine governance. The text, likely composed in Greek in the late Hellenistic period, reflects a profound engagement with Hellenistic philosophical ideas while remaining rooted in the theological context of Judaism. Wisdom of Solomon introduces readers to the personification of wisdom as a divine intermediary and explores themes of immortality, justice, and the relationship between wisdom and the righteous.

Philosophical and Theological Insights

The wisdom literature of Sirach and Wisdom of Solomon encapsulates a harmonious blend of philosophical and theological insights, offering readers a unique vantage point to contemplate the mysteries of life, the divine order, and the pursuit of virtue.

Sirach's philosophical depth lies in its pragmatic approach to ethical living. The author emphasizes the importance of fearing the Lord, honoring parents, and practicing generosity. The ethical teachings of Sirach are grounded in the practical realities of daily life, providing a moral compass for navigating the complexities of human relationships and societal responsibilities. The philosophical underpinnings of Sirach resonate with the classical virtue ethics found in Greco-Roman philosophical traditions, offering a bridge between Jewish wisdom and Hellenistic ethical thought.

Wisdom of Solomon, on the other hand, delves into more abstract and metaphysical realms. The personification of wisdom as a divine emanation reflects a philosophical sophistication that aligns with Hellenistic ideas about the transcendent and the immanent. The text engages with Platonic concepts, portraying wisdom as an eternal and immutable reality that shapes the cosmos. This philosophical integration within Wisdom of Solomon invites readers to contemplate the nature of wisdom beyond the practical and ethical dimensions, delving into the metaphysical currents that underlie the fabric of existence.

Both Sirach and Wisdom of Solomon engage in the exploration of divine providence and theodicy, addressing the age-old question of why the righteous may suffer while the wicked seemingly prosper. Sirach grounds its response in the practical realm, affirming the importance of perseverance, trust in God's justice, and the ultimate reward for the righteous. Wisdom of Solomon, drawing upon its philosophical foundations, unveils a perspective that transcends the temporal realm, affirming the enduring nature of the righteous and the eventual judgment that awaits the wicked.

The theological insights embedded in Sirach and Wisdom of Solomon contribute to the broader understanding of God's presence in the human journey. Sirach emphasizes the covenantal relationship between God and humanity, portraying God as a benevolent guide who invites human cooperation in the pursuit of virtue. Wisdom of Solomon unfolds theological reflections on immortality, presenting a vision of the righteous as those who participate in the divine nature and experience eternal communion with God.

Influence on Christian Ethics

The wisdom literature of Sirach and Wisdom of Solomon has exerted a profound influence on Christian ethics, shaping moral reflection, guiding ethical conduct, and fostering a deeper understanding of the Christian life.

Sirach's impact on Christian ethics is evident in its emphasis on practical virtues and the cultivation of a righteous character. The New Testament echoes Sirach's teachings on humility, forgiveness, and the pursuit of wisdom. Jesus' own ethical teachings, such as the Sermon on the Mount, resonate with the ethical framework laid out in Sirach. The apostolic writings draw upon Sirach's wisdom, incorporating its insights into the ethical exhortations and pastoral guidance offered to early Christian communities.

Wisdom of Solomon contributes to Christian ethics by expanding the theological understanding of the righteous and the consequences of moral choices. The concept of immortality and the participation in divine life found in Wisdom of Solomon resonate with Christian eschatological teachings. The emphasis on the transformative power of wisdom aligns with Pauline theology, where the pursuit of wisdom is intertwined with the Christian journey toward conformity to the image of Christ.

Furthermore, the personification of wisdom in both Sirach and Wisdom of Solomon foreshadows the Christian understanding of Christ as the embodiment of divine wisdom. The prologue of the Gospel of John, with its depiction of Christ as the Word (Logos) through whom all things were made, resonates with the personification of wisdom found in these

Deuterocanonical texts. The influence of Sirach and Wisdom of Solomon on the development of Christological and theological themes within Christianity becomes evident as these texts contribute to the ethical and theological tapestry of Christian thought.

Chapter Thirteen

Tobit, Judith, and Esther

Narrative Characteristics

The narratives of Tobit, Judith, and Esther, nestled within the rich tapestry of the Deuterocanon, unfold as captivating tales that intertwine personal destinies, divine providence, and the triumph of faith. Each book carries distinctive narrative characteristics that contribute to their enduring appeal and canonical significance.

Tobit introduces readers to the pious Tobit, a righteous man of the tribe of Naphtali living in the Assyrian exile. The narrative unfolds with elements of a family drama, as Tobit's commitment to bury the dead and his subsequent blindness set the stage for divine interventions and the journey of his son Tobias. The narrative of Tobit weaves together familial love, angelic encounters, and themes of mercy and justice. The presence of the archangel Raphael, disguised as a fellow traveler, adds a supernatural dimension to Tobit's story, showcasing the interplay between the divine and the human within the intricate fabric of providence.

Judith emerges as a tale of courage and strategic wit, set against the backdrop of the Assyrian siege of Bethulia. The eponymous heroine, Judith, a widow of great beauty and virtue, takes center stage in a narrative marked by suspense, political intrigue, and divine deliverance. Judith's daring act of infiltrating the enemy camp and beheading the Assyrian general Holofernes becomes a symbol of God's intervention through the hands of the unexpected. The narrative of Judith resonates with themes of trust in God's guidance, the subversion of worldly expectations, and the power of righteous actions to alter the course of history.

Esther, situated within the historical context of the Persian Empire, unfolds as a tale of providential deliverance for the Jewish people. The narrative features Esther, a Jewish orphan raised by her cousin Mordecai, who rises to become queen of Persia. The suspenseful plot revolves around Haman's sinister plot to annihilate the Jewish community, and Esther's courageous decision to approach the king uninvited. The narrative of Esther, characterized by intrigue, reversal of fortunes, and the

128

celebration of the festival of Purim, illustrates how divine providence operates through seemingly ordinary individuals to safeguard His people.

Theological Themes

The narratives of Tobit, Judith, and Esther delve into theological themes that resonate with the broader biblical narrative, offering insights into divine providence, the complexities of human agency, and the interplay between faith and deliverance.

The theological theme of divine providence takes center stage in the narrative of Tobit. The angel Raphael, acting as God's messenger, guides and protects Tobit and Tobias throughout their journey. Tobit's unwavering commitment to righteousness, even in the face of personal adversity, becomes a testament to God's providential care for those who trust in Him. The narrative of Tobit affirms the belief that God's hand is active in the details of human lives, orchestrating events for the good of those who remain faithful.

Judith offers theological reflections on the nature of divine deliverance. Judith's courageous act becomes a pivotal moment in the narrative, symbolizing God's intervention in the face of imminent destruction. The narrative emphasizes the role of human agency and trust in God's guidance, illustrating that deliverance often comes through unexpected means. Judith's boldness becomes a paradigm for the belief that God empowers individuals to play essential roles in His redemptive plan.

The theological theme of divine hiddenness pervades the narrative of Esther. Unlike Tobit, where the presence of the angel is explicit, and Judith, where God's deliverance is manifest through Judith's actions, Esther unfolds without direct divine intervention. God's providential work is subtly woven into the events, leaving room for human agency and strategic decisions. The narrative underscores the theological reality that God's presence and providence may not always be conspicuous, yet His guidance shapes the course of history in ways that surpass human comprehension.

Canonical Significance

The canonical significance of Tobit, Judith, and Esther within the Christian Bible emanates from their unique contributions to the broader biblical narrative, their theological depth, and their resonance with Christian ethics and teachings.

Tobit, with its emphasis on righteousness, mercy, and the active presence of divine messengers, aligns with foundational Christian teachings. The narrative's exploration of familial relationships, charity, and the importance of burying the dead adds ethical dimensions that find echoes in the teachings of Jesus. The canonical significance of Tobit lies in its capacity to enrich Christian moral imagination and to emphasize the compassionate aspects of righteous living.

Judith's canonical significance lies in its portrayal of a courageous woman whose actions alter the course of history. The narrative underscores themes of trust in God, the subversion of worldly expectations, and the power of faith-driven actions. Judith's story finds resonance with Christian teachings on courage, faith, and the unexpected avenues through which God's deliverance may manifest. Her canonical place contributes to the Christian understanding of God's sovereignty and the transformative potential of individuals committed to righteousness.

Esther's canonical significance rests on its exploration of divine providence in the absence of explicit divine intervention. The narrative's portrayal of Esther's strategic decisions, Mordecai's wisdom, and the celebration of Purim illuminates the interplay between human agency and divine guidance. Esther's inclusion in the canon enriches Christian theology by presenting a nuanced perspective on how God's providence operates through both the extraordinary and the seemingly mundane.

Chapter Fourteen

Historical Books in the

Deuterocanon

Maccabees and Historical Context

The historical books of Maccabees, within the
Deuterocanon, stand as remarkable narratives that unveil
a pivotal period in Jewish history, marked by political
turmoil, religious resistance, and the quest for freedom.
Comprising 1 Maccabees and 2 Maccabees, these books
provide a detailed account of the Maccabean revolt
against the Seleucid Empire and offer insights into the

struggles and triumphs of the Jewish people during the Hellenistic era.

1 Maccabees unfolds against the backdrop of the Seleucid ruler Antiochus IV's attempts to Hellenize Judea. The narrative centers on the Maccabean family, led by Mattathias and his sons, particularly Judas Maccabeus. The book meticulously details the events leading to the revolt, the military victories, and the rededication of the Temple in Jerusalem—an event commemorated in the festival of Hanukkah. The historical context of 1 Maccabees provides readers with a vivid portrayal of the political machinations, religious persecutions, and the courageous resistance of the Maccabean fighters.

2 Maccabees, while covering some of the same historical events, presents a distinct perspective and style. Written in a more Hellenistic literary tradition, the book offers theological reflections on the events of the Maccabean revolt. 2 Maccabees focuses on the sufferings and martyrdoms of individual Jews, portraying them as heroic witnesses to their faith. The narrative also includes visions and prayers, emphasizing the divine intervention and providence that accompany the struggles of the Jewish people.

Insights into Jewish History

The historical books of Maccabees offer profound insights into a critical juncture of Jewish history, shedding light on the challenges faced by the Jewish community under foreign rule, the resilience of their faith, and the enduring quest for religious freedom.

The Seleucid oppression documented in 1 Maccabees unfolds as a multifaceted assault on Jewish identity and religious practices. Antiochus IV's attempts to Hellenize Judea involved imposing Greek customs, desecrating the Temple, and persecuting those who resisted. The resistance led by the Maccabees becomes a symbol of the unwavering commitment to preserving the Jewish faith against external pressures. The narrative provides a historical lens through which readers can understand the tensions between Hellenistic influences and Jewish religious identity during this period.

2 Maccabees complements the historical account with a focus on individual stories of faith and martyrdom. The book recounts instances of Jews who chose death over violating their religious principles, becoming witnesses to their unwavering commitment to God. These individual narratives provide a personal dimension to the broader historical context, emphasizing the intimate connection between faith and the quest for religious freedom. The historical insights garnered from 2 Maccabees enrich the understanding of the religious and moral convictions that fueled the Maccabean revolt.

The rededication of the Temple, a pivotal event in Maccabean history, is a testament to the resilience of the Jewish spirit. The purification and rededication of the desecrated Temple symbolize the restoration of religious practices and the renewal of Jewish identity. The festival of Hanukkah, instituted to commemorate this event, becomes a perpetual reminder of the triumph of faith over oppression. The insights into Jewish history provided by the Maccabean narratives contribute to a comprehensive understanding of the struggles, victories, and enduring legacy of the Jewish people during this tumultuous period.

Theological Lessons

Embedded within the historical narratives of Maccabees are profound theological lessons that resonate with broader biblical themes, offering insights into divine providence, the relationship between faith and action, and the enduring nature of God's covenant with His people.

The Maccabean narratives affirm the reality of divine providence in the midst of historical turmoil. The victories of the Maccabean forces, against overwhelming odds, are portrayed as acts of divine intervention. The courage and leadership of figures like Judas Maccabeus are depicted as instruments through which God brings about deliverance for His people. The theological underpinning of divine providence in Maccabees echoes the broader biblical narrative, where God's guidance and intervention shape the course of history in accordance with His redemptive purposes.

The Maccabean revolt exemplifies the intertwining of faith and action as essential components of the pursuit of religious freedom. The Maccabees did not merely rely on divine intervention; they actively engaged in military resistance, strategic planning, and courageous leadership. The theological lesson derived from this interplay is that faith, while trusting in God's providence, also involves active participation and commitment to justice. The Maccabean narrative challenges readers to consider the relationship between faith-inspired action and the realization of God's purposes in the world.

The narratives of martyrdom in 2 Maccabees introduce theological reflections on the nature of suffering and fidelity to God's commandments. The martyrs portrayed in the book choose death over compromising their faith, affirming the primacy of loyalty to God even in the face of persecution. The theological lesson drawn from these narratives emphasizes the redemptive nature of suffering and the enduring witness of those who remain faithful to God's covenant. The martyrs become symbols of hope, inspiring subsequent generations to persevere in their commitment to God's truth.

The Maccabean narratives also contribute to the theological understanding of God's covenantal relationship with His people. The rededication of the Temple becomes a tangible expression of the renewal of the covenant, where God's presence is once again acknowledged and revered. The festivals instituted to commemorate these events, such as Hanukkah, become rituals that reinforce the communal remembrance of God's faithfulness and the enduring covenantal bond between God and His people.

Chapter Fifteen

The Deuterocanon's Impact on Christianity

Liturgical Use

The Deuterocanon, though often debated and sometimes marginalized, has played a significant role in shaping Christian liturgical practices, enriching worship traditions, and contributing to the devotional life of believers. While not universally accepted across all Christian denominations, the liturgical use of the Deuterocanonical books has been a source of spiritual nourishment and theological reflection for many.

In liturgical use, certain Christian traditions include readings from the Deuterocanon in their worship services. The inclusion of passages from Tobit, Judith, Wisdom of Solomon, and others provides a broader biblical context for believers, offering a diverse range of narratives, prayers, and theological reflections. The liturgical reading of these books becomes an avenue through which congregations engage with the moral teachings, wisdom literature, and historical narratives unique to the Deuterocanon.

The book of Sirach, for instance, with its practical wisdom and ethical teachings, finds a place in liturgical readings in some traditions. The proverbs and exhortations from Sirach become part of worship services, offering believers insights into righteous living, virtue, and the fear of the Lord. Similarly, the narratives of Tobit and Judith, with their emphasis on faith, deliverance, and divine providence, become integral components of liturgical readings in some Christian communities, contributing to the diversity of biblical themes encountered in worship.

The liturgical use of the Deuterocanon extends beyond mere readings to influence hymnody, prayers, and other elements of worship. Certain hymns draw inspiration from the poetic expressions found in Wisdom literature, echoing themes of divine wisdom, creation, and the search for meaning. The inclusion of prayers inspired by the Deuterocanon reflects a desire to incorporate the rich theological and devotional content these books offer into the worship experience. In this way, the liturgical use of the Deuterocanon becomes a dynamic expression of the multifaceted nature of Christian worship, embracing a broader spectrum of biblical wisdom and narrative.

Doctrinal Development

The impact of the Deuterocanon on doctrinal development within Christianity is multifaceted, contributing to theological reflections on issues such as salvation, ethics, and the nature of God. While not uniformly accepted across all Christian traditions, the doctrinal insights derived from the Deuterocanon have influenced theological discussions and shaped perspectives on Christian faith.

The book of Wisdom of Solomon, for instance, contributes to the development of eschatological thought within Christianity. The emphasis on the immortality of the soul and the idea of the righteous being in the hands of God finds resonance with broader Christian teachings on the afterlife. Although these concepts are not explicit in other canonical books, the Wisdom of Solomon provides a lens through which believers engage with questions of eternal life and the destiny of the righteous.

The inclusion of the Deuterocanon in certain Christian traditions has also impacted discussions on justification and salvation. The book of Tobit, with its emphasis on acts of charity and righteousness, has influenced reflections on the relationship between faith and works. While the Protestant Reformation placed a distinctive emphasis on justification by faith alone, the inclusion of Tobit in the Catholic and Eastern Orthodox canons has contributed to nuanced discussions about the synergy between faith and works within Christian soteriology.

Moreover, the theological reflections on divine mercy, justice, and providence found in the Deuterocanon have informed Christian doctrines concerning the nature of God. The narratives of Judith and Esther, for instance, highlight the theme of divine intervention in human affairs, portraying God as a protector and deliverer of His people. These theological insights contribute to a more holistic understanding of God's character, influencing discussions on divine attributes and the relationship between God and His creation.

While the doctrinal impact of the Deuterocanon varies across Christian traditions, its influence is particularly pronounced in the formulation of doctrines within the Catholic and Eastern Orthodox traditions. The teachings and theological perspectives embedded in the Deuterocanon continue to be a rich source for theological reflection and doctrinal development within the broader tapestry of Christian faith.

Ecumenical Perspectives

The inclusion of the Deuterocanon in certain Christian canons has been a source of ecumenical perspectives and, at times, a point of divergence among Christian denominations. The varying acceptance of these books has contributed to discussions surrounding the canon of Scripture and the principles guiding its determination.

While the Deuterocanon is considered canonical by the Catholic and Eastern Orthodox Churches, Protestant denominations typically regard these books as apocryphal.

The divergent views on the Deuterocanon have sparked theological dialogues and reflections on the criteria for canonization. Historical considerations, including the process of transmission and acceptance of certain books in specific Christian traditions, have played a role in shaping ecumenical perspectives. The dialogues surrounding the canon have prompted Christians to reflect on the authority of tradition, the role of Church councils, and the development of the biblical canon within different ecclesiastical contexts.

Liturgical encounters have also served as spaces for ecumenical engagement around the Deuterocanon. While certain Christian denominations include readings from these books in their worship services, others may not. Ecumenical discussions on the liturgical use of the Deuterocanon provide an opportunity for believers from different traditions to engage with the richness of these texts, fostering mutual understanding and theological dialogue.

Furthermore, the Deuterocanon serves as a locus for theological exchange among Christian traditions. The divergent theological emphases within these books, such as the role of works in salvation or the nature of intercession, become points for theological reflection and discussion. While these discussions may not always lead to doctrinal convergence, they contribute to a deeper understanding of the theological diversity within the Christian family and encourage believers to engage with perspectives beyond their own theological traditions.

PART IV: Pseudepigrapha -

Unveiling Hidden Texts

Chapter Sixteen

Introduction to Pseudepigrapha

Defining Pseudepigraphical Writings

The term "pseudepigrapha" encompasses a diverse collection of ancient Jewish and Christian writings that claim authorship by notable figures from the past, often prophets or other revered individuals. The word itself, derived from Greek roots meaning "false writings" or "writings with false superscriptions," reflects the central characteristic of these texts—the attribution of authorship to someone other than the actual writer. Pseudepigrapha emerged within the cultural and religious milieu of Second Temple Judaism and early

Christianity, presenting a unique literary genre with distinct features.

The diversity of pseudepigraphical writings is notable, ranging from apocalyptic visions and wisdom literature to historical narratives and prayers. Examples include the Book of Enoch, the Apocalypse of Moses, the Testament of the Twelve Patriarchs, and the Assumption of Moses. These texts often claim to reveal hidden knowledge, foretell future events, or provide insights into divine mysteries. The attribution of authorship to revered figures of the past lends an aura of authority and authenticity to these writings, making them influential within certain religious circles.

While the pseudepigrapha is not a monolithic category, scholars often classify these writings into Old Testament Pseudepigrapha (OT Pseudep) and New Testament Pseudepigrapha (NT Pseudep), based on their presumed connection to either the Hebrew Scriptures or the Christian New Testament. The Book of Enoch and the Apocalypse of Moses, for instance, fall into the former category, while the Gospel of Thomas and the Apocalypse of Peter belong to the latter.

Authorship Controversies

One of the defining characteristics of pseudepigrapha is the inherent authorship controversies surrounding these texts. Unlike canonical writings, where authorship is typically clear and attributed to recognized figures, pseudepigraphical works intentionally adopt pseudonyms to lend authority and authenticity to their message. The names of Enoch, Moses, Solomon, and other revered figures from biblical history frequently appear as supposed authors of these writings.

The use of pseudonyms serves multiple purposes within the pseudepigrapha. Firstly, it establishes a direct connection with the authoritative figures of the past, lending weight to the teachings or revelations presented in the text. The pseudonymous attribution implies that the content is not merely the product of human speculation but represents divine truths revealed to esteemed figures in antiquity. This intentional association with revered personalities elevates the status of the pseudepigrapha within religious communities.

Secondly, the use of pseudonyms creates a sense of continuity with the existing biblical canon. By attributing a writing to a figure like Enoch or Moses, authors of pseudepigrapha position their texts as extensions of the authoritative tradition found in the Hebrew Scriptures. This continuity enhances the perceived legitimacy of their message and positions the pseudepigrapha within the broader context of divine revelation.

However, these authorship claims also raise significant controversies, both historically and in contemporary scholarly discussions. The intentional use of pseudonyms challenges conventional notions of authorship and raises questions about the ethical implications of such practices. In modern terms, these writings might be deemed as forgeries, yet understanding them within their historical and religious context is crucial for a nuanced appreciation of their significance.

Historical Context

To comprehend the emergence of pseudepigrapha, it is essential to delve into the historical context of Second Temple Judaism and early Christianity. The period between the fifth century BCE and the second century CE witnessed profound cultural, religious, and political transformations, providing a fertile ground for the development of pseudepigraphical writings.

In Second Temple Judaism, the exile in Babylon and subsequent returns to Jerusalem shaped the religious identity of the Jewish community. The prophetic tradition, already significant in pre-exilic times, gained prominence as a means of interpreting and understanding the experiences of exile, return, and the challenges faced by the Jewish people. Pseudepigrapha, with its pseudonymous attributions to ancient prophets, taps into this prophetic tradition, offering new revelations and interpretations of divine mysteries.

The Hellenistic influence on the Jewish world during this period also played a crucial role in shaping the context for pseudepigraphical writings. The encounter with Greek philosophy, literature, and religious ideas spurred a reevaluation of Jewish traditions and beliefs. Pseudepigrapha, with its fusion of Jewish and Hellenistic thought, reflects the dynamic nature of cultural exchange during this time. The Book of Wisdom, for instance, exhibits influences from Greek philosophical ideas while exploring themes of divine wisdom within a Jewish context.

The apocalyptic fervor of the Second Temple period, characterized by an intense expectation of divine intervention, the coming of the Messiah, and the establishment of God's kingdom, further contributed to the proliferation of pseudepigraphical works. The apocalyptic genre, which often explored visions, cosmic battles, and the unveiling of hidden truths, found expression in writings like the Book of Enoch and the Apocalypse of Moses.

Within early Christianity, the historical context of theological diversity and the formation of the New Testament canon also played a role in the development of pseudepigraphical writings. As Christian communities grappled with theological questions, Christological debates, and diverse interpretations of the life and teachings of Jesus, some sought to bolster their perspectives by attributing writings to apostles or other prominent figures from the apostolic era. The Gospel of Thomas, the Apocalypse of Peter, and other texts emerged in this context, claiming connections to authoritative figures within the early Christian community.

Chapter Seventeen

Enochian Pseudepigrapha

Expansion of Enochian Tradition

The Enochian Pseudepigrapha represents a fascinating and intricate corpus of writings that expands upon the Enochian tradition initiated by the biblical figure Enoch. The Book of Enoch, also known as 1 Enoch, laid the foundation for a rich tapestry of literature that delves into visionary experiences, celestial realms, and profound theological insights. The Enochian Pseudepigrapha extends this tradition, offering diverse perspectives on the enigmatic figure of Enoch and his interactions with heavenly realms.

Within the Enochian Pseudepigrapha, various works like the Second Book of Enoch (2 Enoch or Slavonic Enoch), the Third Book of Enoch (3 Enoch or Hebrew Enoch), and the Secrets of Enoch present expanded narratives and elaborate cosmologies that build upon the glimpses provided in the canonical Book of Enoch. These writings contribute to the development of Enochian mysticism, providing readers with a more detailed exploration of Enoch's encounters with angels, his heavenly journeys, and his reception of divine revelations.

The expansion of the Enochian tradition within the pseudepigrapha serves multiple purposes. Firstly, it deepens the exploration of Enoch's role as a mediator between heaven and earth. The expanded narratives portray Enoch not merely as a righteous figure who walked with God, as presented in Genesis, but as an elevated being granted access to celestial mysteries. The revelations in these writings go beyond the canonical account, detailing Enoch's journeys through various heavenly realms, encounters with angelic beings, and the reception of esoteric knowledge.

Secondly, the Enochian Pseudepigrapha contributes to the understanding of cosmic hierarchies and the celestial order. These works introduce readers to intricate depictions of angelic realms, the functions of different angelic orders, and the cosmic geography of heaven. The cosmological insights found in the Enochian Pseudepigrapha offer readers a broader perspective on the spiritual dimensions of the universe, emphasizing the interconnectedness between the earthly and heavenly realms.

Moreover, the expansion of the Enochian tradition in these writings serves as a theological bridge between the Old and New Testaments. The Enochian Pseudepigrapha, with its elaborate depictions of messianic figures and eschatological visions, contributes to the broader narrative of salvation history. The anticipation of a messianic figure, often referred to as the Son of Man, aligns with similar expectations found in both Jewish and early Christian thought, creating a continuity that spans across the biblical canon and the pseudepigraphical writings.

Theological Diversity

The Enochian Pseudepigrapha exhibits a remarkable theological diversity that reflects the dynamic and multifaceted nature of Enochian mysticism. Unlike a monolithic theological perspective, these writings present a spectrum of ideas, themes, and theological emphases that contribute to a nuanced understanding of Enochian traditions.

One theological theme that permeates the Enochian Pseudepigrapha is the concept of divine judgment and the destinies of the righteous and the wicked. The apocalyptic visions contained in these writings often depict a cosmic judgment scene where the deeds of individuals are weighed, and their fates are determined. The diverse perspectives on eschatology within the

Enochian Pseudepigrapha provide readers with a range of theological reflections on the ultimate purpose of human existence and the divine plan for salvation.

Furthermore, the Enochian Pseudepigrapha introduces readers to various angelic beings, each with specific roles and functions in the cosmic order. The diversity of angels, archangels, and other celestial entities reflects the intricate hierarchy that governs the heavenly realms. This theological exploration of angelology contributes to a more comprehensive understanding of the spiritual beings that populate the Enochian tradition and their roles in mediating divine messages to humanity.

The theme of wisdom is another theological thread woven into the Enochian Pseudepigrapha. Wisdom literature, characterized by its emphasis on moral instruction and the pursuit of divine knowledge, is present in works like the Book of Wisdom of Solomon and certain sections of 2 Enoch. The quest for wisdom, often personified as a divine figure, becomes a central theme that aligns with broader biblical wisdom literature and resonates with the pursuit of understanding and righteousness.

Moreover, the Enochian Pseudepigrapha contributes to the theological exploration of the divine nature. While the canonical Book of Enoch introduces the concept of the "Son of Man" as a messianic figure, the pseudepigraphical writings further elaborate on this divine figure's role in the cosmic drama of redemption. The diverse theological perspectives on the nature and identity of the "Son of Man" provide readers with a rich tapestry of reflections on the relationship between the divine and the human within the Enochian tradition.

Comparative Analysis

A comparative analysis of the Enochian Pseudepigrapha reveals both continuity and diversity in theological themes when compared to the canonical Book of Enoch and other biblical writings. The expansion of the Enochian tradition in the pseudepigrapha maintains continuity with the foundational narrative of Enoch's righteous walk with God and his privileged access to divine revelations. However, it also introduces new theological dimensions that contribute to a more intricate understanding of Enochian mysticism.

The concept of celestial journeys and visions, present in the canonical Book of Enoch, finds further elaboration and expansion in the pseudepigraphical works. The narratives within the Enochian Pseudepigrapha offer readers a more detailed exploration of Enoch's experiences in heavenly realms, encounters with angelic beings, and revelations of divine mysteries. This expansion deepens the mystical and visionary aspects of the Enochian tradition, providing a more immersive theological experience for readers.

Additionally, the Enochian Pseudepigrapha demonstrates a theological flexibility that accommodates diverse perspectives on eschatology, angelology, and the nature of the divine. While the canonical Book of Enoch sets the groundwork for certain theological themes, the pseudepigraphical works explore these themes with a greater degree of variation. This theological diversity allows readers to engage with different theological perspectives within the broader context of Enochian mysticism.

The comparative analysis also reveals a thematic continuity with broader biblical traditions. The anticipation of a messianic figure, the exploration of wisdom as a divine attribute, and the emphasis on divine judgment align with themes found in both Old and New Testament writings. The Enochian Pseudepigrapha, despite its unique theological expressions, contributes to the broader theological tapestry of biblical literature.

In conclusion, the Enochian Pseudepigrapha represents a remarkable expansion and elaboration of the Enochian tradition, offering readers an intricate theological exploration of Enoch's role, celestial realms, and divine revelations. The theological diversity within these writings reflects the dynamic nature of Enochian mysticism, providing readers with a nuanced understanding of eschatology, angelology, and the divine nature. The comparative analysis highlights both continuity and variation in theological themes, inviting readers to delve into the rich theological tapestry of the Enochian Pseudepigrapha within the broader context of biblical literature.

Chapter Eighteen

Other Notable

Pseudepigraphical Texts

Ascension of Isaiah

The Ascension of Isaiah stands as a distinctive pseudepigraphical text within the broader landscape of ancient writings. Composed in two parts, the first dating from the late Second Temple period and the second likely from the early Christian era, this work provides readers with a captivating narrative that blends apocalyptic visions, angelic encounters, and messianic expectations.

The first part of the Ascension of Isaiah unveils a series of visions granted to the prophet Isaiah, spanning from the earthly realm to the highest heavens. Isaiah's ascent through the celestial spheres serves as a conduit for divine revelations concerning the future fate of Israel, the advent of a messianic figure, and cosmic battles between angelic forces and demonic powers. The vivid imagery and cosmic scope of these visions contribute to the apocalyptic character of the text, aligning it with other apocalyptic writings of its time.

The second part of the Ascension of Isaiah shifts its focus to the earthly life of Jesus Christ, presenting a unique perspective on the Incarnation, crucifixion, and resurrection. Within this narrative framework, Isaiah, now living in the earthly realm, witnesses the events of Jesus' life unfold. The text emphasizes the hidden nature of Christ's divinity during his earthly sojourn, his descent into the realm of the dead, and his triumphant ascent back to the heavenly spheres. This distinctive portrayal of Christ's earthly life and divine nature sets the Ascension of Isaiah apart from other New Testament narratives.

Implications for Christian Theology

The Ascension of Isaiah holds significant implications for Christian theology, particularly in its unique perspectives on the nature of Christ and the cosmic drama of salvation. The dual nature of Christ, as both fully divine and fully human, finds nuanced expression in this text. The first part underscores the transcendence of the messianic figure, linking him to celestial realms and divine prerogatives. Meanwhile, the second part emphasizes the incarnation of the divine into human flesh, offering a distinctive narrative of Jesus' earthly life and the salvific significance of his death and resurrection.

Furthermore, the Ascension of Isaiah contributes to the broader Christian understanding of the atonement. The text's portrayal of Christ's descent into the realm of the dead and subsequent ascent to the heavenly spheres provides a unique lens through which to interpret the redemptive impact of Christ's sacrifice. The narrative suggests a cosmic victory over demonic forces and the liberation of souls from the power of death, aligning with

Pauline and Johannine themes of Christ's triumph over sin and death.

In addition, the Ascension of Isaiah provides a bridge between Old Testament prophecies and New Testament fulfillment. The incorporation of Isaiah, a revered figure from the Hebrew Scriptures, into the narrative of Christ's life underscores the continuity of God's plan throughout salvation history. The text weaves together strands of messianic expectations from the prophetic tradition with the fulfillment of those expectations in the person of Jesus Christ, offering readers a unique synthesis of Old and New Testament perspectives.

In conclusion, the Ascension of Isaiah emerges as a noteworthy pseudepigraphical text that engages readers with apocalyptic visions, celestial realms, and a distinctive portrayal of the life of Jesus Christ. Its implications for Christian theology extend to the understanding of Christ's dual nature, the cosmic drama of salvation, and the continuity between Old and New Testament revelations. As readers delve into the Ascension of Isaiah, they encounter a narrative that enriches their theological perspectives and invites contemplation on the profound mysteries of the divine plan.

Testament of Abraham

The Testament of Abraham stands as a compelling and enigmatic pseudepigraphical work that offers readers a glimpse into the life and spiritual journey of the patriarch Abraham. Composed in a narrative style, this text purports to be a testament or farewell discourse delivered by Abraham himself before his death. Through a series of vivid visions and dialogues with divine beings, the Testament of Abraham explores themes of faith, righteousness, and the nature of the divine.

The narrative unfolds with Abraham receiving a summons from the Archangel Michael to ascend into the heavenly realms. This ascent serves as the backdrop for the profound visions and encounters that follow. Within the celestial spheres, Abraham engages in dialogues with various angelic beings, including the Archangel Michael, who serves as his guide and instructor. These dialogues delve into theological inquiries about the nature of God, the destiny of souls, and the dynamics of the spiritual realm.

A central theme within the Testament of Abraham is the exploration of Abraham's righteousness and faithfulness. The text portrays Abraham as a paragon of virtue, a model of unwavering devotion to God. The patriarch's moral integrity and deep trust in the divine are highlighted through his interactions with celestial beings and his commitment to fulfill God's commands, even when faced with challenging and ethically complex situations.

Implications for Christian Theology

The Testament of Abraham holds implications for Christian theology, particularly in its exploration of themes related to faith, righteousness, and the nature of the divine. The text contributes to the broader understanding of Abraham as a foundational figure in the Abrahamic traditions, drawing connections between the patriarch's virtues and Christian theological perspectives.

Abraham's unwavering faith becomes a focal point within the narrative, aligning with biblical accounts of Abraham's trust in God's promises. The Testament of Abraham emphasizes the patriarch's willingness to sacrifice his son Isaac, presenting it as a supreme act of obedience and devotion. This narrative element resonates with the Abrahamic faith tradition and finds echoes in Christian theological reflections on faith as exemplified in figures like Abraham.

Moreover, the celestial dialogues within the Testament of Abraham delve into theological inquiries about the nature of God and the destiny of souls. The text engages with questions about divine justice, the afterlife, and the role of angelic beings in the cosmic order. These theological explorations offer readers insights into the spiritual dimensions of existence and contribute to the broader discussion on the nature of the divine in Christian thought.

The Testament of Abraham also addresses eschatological themes, providing a glimpse into the fate of souls after death. The celestial journey of Abraham and the visions of the heavenly realms contribute to the text's apocalyptic character, offering readers a perspective on the ultimate destiny of the righteous and the consequences for those who deviate from the path of righteousness. This eschatological dimension aligns with broader biblical and apocalyptic traditions, enriching Christian theological perspectives on the afterlife.

Chapter Nineteen

Literary Styles in Pseudepigrapha

Apocalyptic and Wisdom Literature

The Pseudepigrapha encompasses a diverse array of literary styles, each contributing to a tapestry of ancient Jewish and early Christian writings. Two prominent literary styles within the Pseudepigrapha are apocalyptic and wisdom literature. These distinctive genres not only showcase the creativity of ancient authors but also offer readers profound insights into theological, eschatological, and philosophical dimensions.

- **Apocalyptic Literature**

Apocalyptic literature within the Pseudepigrapha is characterized by its visionary nature, cosmic imagery, and revelatory content. Works such as the Book of Enoch, the Apocalypse of Abraham, and the Ascension of Isaiah exemplify this genre. Apocalyptic writings often claim to reveal hidden knowledge about the divine plan, the nature of the cosmos, and the future. The visionary experiences of the authors, often depicted as journeys through celestial realms, serve as a vehicle for unveiling mysteries beyond the scope of ordinary human understanding.

The apocalyptic style is marked by its emphasis on eschatological themes, including the coming of a messianic figure, divine judgment, and the ultimate fate of the righteous and the wicked. Symbolic language and vivid imagery are integral to conveying these profound truths. Celestial visions, encounters with angelic beings, and symbolic numbers contribute to the intricate tapestry of apocalyptic literature, inviting readers to contemplate the cosmic drama of salvation.

Moreover, apocalyptic writings frequently address the tension between good and evil, depicting cosmic battles between angelic forces and demonic powers. The Book of Enoch, for instance, introduces readers to the Watchers, fallen angels who corrupt humanity, leading to divine judgment and the eventual triumph of righteousness. This cosmic struggle reflects the apocalyptic worldview's dualistic understanding of cosmic forces at play in the unfolding drama of redemption.

- **Wisdom Literature**

In contrast to the visionary and cosmic nature of apocalyptic literature, wisdom literature within the Pseudepigrapha emphasizes moral and ethical teachings, philosophical reflections, and the pursuit of divine knowledge. Works such as the Wisdom of Solomon, the Wisdom of Sirach (Ecclesiasticus), and the Testament of Solomon fall within this genre. Wisdom literature often takes the form of proverbial sayings, poetic hymns, and reflective discourses that guide readers in leading virtuous lives.

The wisdom tradition, rooted in the pursuit of divine wisdom, explores fundamental questions about the nature of God, the purpose of human existence, and the moral order of the universe. The Wisdom of Solomon, for example, reflects on the immortality of the soul, the justice of God, and the righteous path to wisdom. The teachings within wisdom literature often serve as ethical guides, providing readers with practical insights into virtuous living and the pursuit of divine understanding.

Moreover, wisdom literature engages with philosophical inquiries, contemplating the nature of good and evil, the consequences of moral choices, and the complexities of human existence. The Book of Sirach, with its pragmatic advice on various aspects of life, addresses the challenges of human relationships, the pursuit of knowledge, and the cultivation of virtue. The wisdom tradition, characterized by its focus on discernment and ethical instruction, offers readers a valuable resource for navigating the complexities of life.

Narrative Techniques

The Pseudepigrapha employs a variety of narrative techniques to convey its theological, historical, and ethical messages. While the primary focus is often on the content of the narratives, the methods of storytelling within these texts contribute to their overall impact and resonance with readers.

- **Interweaving of Visions and Dialogue**

Many pseudepigraphical texts, especially those of an apocalyptic nature, utilize the technique of interweaving visions and dialogues. The Book of Enoch, for instance, unfolds through a series of visions granted to Enoch, accompanied by dialogues with angelic beings. This narrative technique not only conveys the visionary experiences of the protagonist but also provides opportunities for theological insights and revelations to be delivered through divine or angelic discourse.

The interplay between visions and dialogues creates a dynamic narrative structure, allowing readers to engage with both the experiential and intellectual dimensions of the text. The visionary sequences offer vivid and symbolic depictions of cosmic realities, while the dialogues provide interpretative frameworks and theological explanations. This narrative technique enhances the immersive quality of the storytelling, inviting readers into the mystical and intellectual realms of the text.

Symbolic Imagery and Allegory

Symbolic imagery and allegory are integral narrative techniques employed within the Pseudepigrapha. These techniques allow authors to convey complex theological concepts, cosmic realities, and moral lessons through vivid and metaphorical language. The Apocalypse of Abraham, for example, utilizes allegorical visions to depict the fate of souls and the nature of divine judgment.

In the Book of Enoch, the use of symbolic imagery is evident in the descriptions of celestial realms, angelic beings, and cosmic events. The symbolism employed, such as the imagery of stars, heavenly tablets, and cosmic journeys, serves as a means of communicating profound truths beyond the limitations of literal language. This technique invites readers to engage in interpretative reflection, unraveling the layers of meaning embedded in the symbolic tapestry of the text.

Moreover, allegorical storytelling allows authors to address theological and ethical themes in a nuanced manner. The Testament of Abraham, for instance, utilizes allegory to convey profound truths about faith, sacrifice, and the nature of God. The narrative of Abraham's celestial journey becomes a vehicle for exploring complex theological concepts through a story that resonates with readers on both emotional and intellectual levels.

Chapter Twenty

Pseudepigrapha in Early Christian Thought

Reception and Influence

The reception and influence of the Pseudepigrapha in early Christian thought constitute a fascinating chapter in the development of Christian theology. As the nascent Christian community grappled with theological questions and sought to understand the significance of the life and teachings of Jesus Christ, various non-canonical texts, including those found in the

Pseudepigrapha, played a role in shaping doctrinal perspectives and influencing theological discourse.

One significant aspect of the reception of Pseudepigraphical writings was their use in Christian communities for edification and instruction. While not included in the canonical Scriptures, texts such as the Book of Enoch and the Wisdom of Solomon found readership among early Christians. These writings, with their apocalyptic visions and wisdom teachings, provided additional insights into cosmic realities, the nature of God, and the ethical dimensions of Christian living.

Moreover, some Pseudepigrapha were regarded as authoritative by certain Christian groups. For instance, the Book of Enoch held a place of significance in early Christian communities, with some considering it a source of divine revelation. The influence of such texts is evident in the writings of early Christian theologians, who drew upon Pseudepigraphical ideas to articulate their theological perspectives and understandings of salvation.

Disputes and Councils

The reception of Pseudepigrapha in early Christian thought was not without controversy. Disputes arose within the Christian community regarding the status and authority of non-canonical texts. The divergent views on the acceptance of certain Pseudepigrapha led to debates and discussions that shaped the trajectory of Christian orthodoxy.

One notable example is the controversy surrounding the Book of Enoch. While some early Christian theologians acknowledged its influence and drew upon its ideas, others expressed reservations about its canonical status. The divergence in opinion on the authoritative nature of Pseudepigraphical writings contributed to theological disputes within the early Church.

The need to address such disputes and establish doctrinal clarity led to the convening of ecumenical councils. The Councils of Hippo and Carthage in the fourth and fifth centuries sought to delineate the canon of Scripture, identifying authoritative texts for Christian doctrine. In this process, certain Pseudepigrapha were excluded from the recognized canon, solidifying the boundaries of orthodoxy within the Christian tradition.

Legacy in Christian Theology

Despite the disputes and decisions regarding canonical status, the legacy of Pseudepigrapha in Christian theology endured. The ideas and themes found in these non-canonical writings continued to influence theological discussions, even among those texts officially excluded from the canon. The legacy of Pseudepigrapha in early Christian thought can be observed in several key areas.

- **Apocalyptic Eschatology**

The apocalyptic visions and eschatological themes present in Pseudepigrapha had a lasting impact on Christian theology. Although some texts were excluded from the canon, their influence on early Christian eschatology persisted. Ideas about the coming of a messianic figure, divine judgment, and the cosmic drama of salvation found resonance in later Christian writings.

Notable early Christian theologians, such as Augustine of Hippo, engaged with apocalyptic themes in their theological reflections. While formulating their views on the end times and the nature of Christ's return, they drew upon the rich imagery and visionary language present in Pseudepigraphical writings. The legacy of apocalyptic eschatology from the Pseudepigrapha thus continued to shape Christian theological perspectives.

- **Ethical and Wisdom Teachings**

The ethical and wisdom teachings found in Pseudepigraphical writings also left an enduring imprint on Christian theology. The Wisdom of Solomon, for example, contributed to discussions on the pursuit of divine wisdom and the moral dimensions of human existence. Although not included in the canon, these teachings influenced Christian ethical reflection and discussions on the role of wisdom in the Christian life.

The legacy of Pseudepigraphical wisdom teachings can be traced in the works of Christian theologians who grappled with questions of virtue, righteous living, and the pursuit of divine knowledge. The ethical insights present in these non-canonical texts resonated with broader Christian discussions on the moral dimensions of the Christian journey.

- **Christological Reflections**

Certain Pseudepigrapha, despite their non-canonical status, contributed to early Christological reflections. The influence of ideas surrounding the pre-existence of Christ, his cosmic significance, and his role in the divine plan can be discerned in the writings of theologians who engaged with Pseudepigraphical themes.

While formulating doctrines related to the nature of Christ, the early Church Fathers grappled with concepts present in non-canonical texts. The legacy of Pseudepigrapha in shaping early Christological discussions underscores the nuanced interplay between canonical and non-canonical writings in the development of Christian theology.

PART V: Theological

Reflections on the Apocrypha

Chapter Twenty One

Apocrypha and Christian

Doctrine

Doctrinal Harmony and Dissonance

The interaction between the Apocrypha and Christian doctrine has been marked by both doctrinal harmony and dissonance within the history of Christianity. The Apocrypha, a collection of texts not found in the canonical Scriptures of most Protestant denominations, includes books that have been part of the Christian tradition for centuries. The doctrinal status of these books, however, varies among Christian denominations, leading to both points of agreement and divergence within Christian theology.

In certain Christian traditions, such as the Roman Catholic and Eastern Orthodox Churches, the Apocrypha holds a recognized and authoritative position within the canon. These additional books, which include Tobit, Judith, Wisdom of Solomon, Sirach (Ecclesiasticus), Baruch, and others, are considered deuterocanonical. The doctrinal harmony in these traditions arises from the acceptance of these books as Scripture, leading to their incorporation into liturgical practices, theological reflections, and moral teachings. The deuterocanonical books contribute to a more comprehensive understanding of Christian doctrine in these traditions.

On the other hand, many Protestant denominations exclude the Apocrypha from their official canon, considering these texts as valuable for historical and literary purposes but not authoritative for doctrinal formulation. The doctrinal dissonance emerges as different Christian traditions emphasize certain books while omitting others, reflecting historical and theological distinctions in their understanding of the Bible's composition and authority.

Theological Reflections

The Apocrypha has played a significant role in shaping theological reflections within Christian traditions that include these books in their canon. The doctrinal content found in the Apocrypha encompasses diverse theological themes that contribute to the broader tapestry of Christian thought.

- **Salvation and Eschatology**

The deuterocanonical books engage with themes related to salvation and eschatology, providing theological reflections on the destiny of the righteous and the nature of God's redemptive plan. Wisdom of Solomon, for example, contemplates the immortality of the soul and the rewards reserved for the righteous in the afterlife. These reflections contribute to a nuanced understanding of salvation and eschatological hope within the context of Christian theology.

Moreover, the inclusion of the Book of Maccabees in certain canons adds historical and theological dimensions to discussions on martyrdom and the resurrection of the dead. The theological reflections found in the Apocrypha enrich Christian perspectives on the ultimate purpose of human existence and the divine fulfillment of God's redemptive promises.

- **Moral and Ethical Teachings**

The Apocrypha also contains valuable moral and ethical teachings that have influenced theological reflections on virtuous living within the Christian tradition. Sirach (Ecclesiasticus), for instance, provides practical wisdom on various aspects of life, including relationships, work, and personal conduct. The moral and ethical guidance within the Apocrypha complements similar teachings found in the canonical Scriptures, offering additional insights into the Christian understanding of righteous living.

The inclusion of Judith, with its narrative of courage and faithfulness, provides a model for ethical decision-making and loyalty to God. These moral and ethical teachings within the Apocrypha contribute to the development of Christian virtue and the application of biblical principles to daily life.

Influence on Contemporary Christianity

The influence of the Apocrypha on contemporary Christianity extends beyond theological reflections to impact liturgical practices, artistic expressions, and ethical considerations within Christian communities.

- **Liturgy and Devotion**

In Christian traditions that include the Apocrypha in their canon, these books have influenced liturgical practices and devotional life. The Wisdom of Solomon and Sirach, with their wisdom teachings, find resonance in liturgical readings and sermons, providing spiritual nourishment for believers. The inclusion of Tobias and Judith in liturgical celebrations adds narrative richness to the Christian worship experience.

Moreover, certain prayers and hymns drawn from the Apocrypha are incorporated into the worship traditions of churches that recognize these texts as authoritative. This liturgical integration reflects the enduring impact of the Apocrypha on the devotional life of Christian communities.

- Artistic and Cultural Expressions

The Apocrypha has also inspired artistic expressions and cultural representations within Christianity. The narratives found in Tobit, Judith, and Maccabees, for example, have been depicted in visual arts, literature, and music. The stories of courageous figures like Judith and the Maccabean martyrs have inspired creative works that celebrate faithfulness, resilience, and divine intervention.

The influence of the Apocrypha extends to Christian literature, where authors draw upon these texts for inspiration and thematic exploration. The characters and narratives from the Apocrypha become sources of reflection on human nature, divine providence, and the complexities of faith, contributing to the broader cultural legacy of Christian storytelling.

- **Ethical Considerations**

The Apocrypha continues to contribute to ethical considerations within contemporary Christianity. The moral teachings found in books like Sirach provide a resource for addressing contemporary ethical challenges. Christian ethicists may draw upon the wisdom literature of the Apocrypha to engage with issues related to justice, integrity, and compassionate living.

Furthermore, the ethical dilemmas faced by characters in the narratives of the Apocrypha offer valuable insights for ethical reflection within Christian communities. The stories of individuals navigating complex situations with faith and courage become a source of guidance for contemporary believers seeking to live out their faith in the complexities of the modern world.

Chapter Twenty

Apocrypha and Eschatology

Apocalyptic Themes

The Apocrypha, a collection of ancient texts that hold diverse theological insights, significantly contributes to the rich tapestry of eschatological themes within Christian thought. These apocalyptic themes, often characterized by visions of the end times, divine judgment, and the cosmic drama of salvation, are interwoven throughout various books in the Apocrypha.

One notable example is the Book of Enoch, a text that delves into profound apocalyptic visions and cosmic mysteries. The apocalyptic themes within Enochic literature provide a glimpse into the divine realms, offering a framework for understanding the unfolding of God's plan for humanity. The celestial journeys and visions of heavenly realms in Enoch contribute to eschatological perspectives, shaping Christian beliefs about the ultimate destiny of the soul and the culmination of God's redemptive purposes.

The Wisdom of Solomon, another book within the Apocrypha, engages with apocalyptic themes by exploring the fate of the righteous and the wicked in the afterlife. This wisdom literature reflects on the divine justice that awaits individuals in the eschatological context, providing a nuanced understanding of the consequences of human actions beyond earthly life.

Eschatological Perspectives

The Apocrypha offers diverse eschatological perspectives that enrich the broader Christian understanding of the end times. These perspectives encompass a range of themes, including resurrection, divine judgment, and the establishment of God's eternal kingdom.

- **Resurrection and Afterlife**

Eschatological perspectives within the Apocrypha contribute to the Christian understanding of resurrection and the afterlife. The Book of Tobit, for instance, addresses themes of divine healing and restoration. The narrative depicts the angel Raphael guiding Tobias, the protagonist, on a journey of faith, culminating in the healing of Tobit's blindness. This restorative theme resonates with eschatological hope, symbolizing the anticipation of spiritual healing and renewal in the ultimate consummation of God's redemptive plan.

.

Similarly, the Second Book of Maccabees provides accounts of martyrs who faced persecution for their faith. The eschatological perspective in these narratives emphasizes the resurrection of the righteous, affirming the hope that even in the face of earthly suffering, believers can anticipate a future resurrection and participation in God's eternal kingdom.

- **Divine Judgment and Justice**

Eschatological perspectives within the Apocrypha also delve into the concepts of divine judgment and justice. The Wisdom of Solomon reflects on the righteous judgment that awaits individuals in the afterlife, highlighting the moral dimensions of eschatological beliefs. This emphasis on divine justice shapes Christian perspectives on ethical living, emphasizing the significance of moral conduct in light of the eschatological realities portrayed in the Apocrypha.

The inclusion of the Book of Judith in certain canons further contributes to eschatological reflections on divine justice. The narrative of Judith, a courageous woman who delivers her people from an oppressive enemy, portrays the theme of divine intervention and the ultimate triumph of God's justice. This eschatological perspective underscores the belief that, in the face of adversity, God's justice will prevail, providing hope and assurance for believers.

Impact on Christian End-Times Beliefs

The Apocrypha's impact on Christian end-times beliefs is profound, influencing theological reflections, liturgical practices, and popular understandings of the final consummation of God's plan. The apocalyptic and eschatological themes found in the Apocrypha contribute to the broader theological landscape of Christian beliefs about the end times.

- **Theological Reflections on the End Times**

The inclusion of apocryphal books in certain Christian canons has led to theological reflections that incorporate eschatological themes from these texts. The Book of Enoch, despite its disputed canonical status, has influenced Christian theology, particularly in traditions that recognize its significance. The apocalyptic visions and celestial journeys in Enochic literature contribute to theological reflections on the cosmic dimensions of eschatology, emphasizing the role of divine revelation in shaping beliefs about the end times.

Moreover, the Wisdom of Solomon's exploration of the fate of the righteous and the wicked in the afterlife informs theological discussions on divine judgment and the ultimate destiny of human souls. The impact of these eschatological perspectives extends to Christian doctrines related to salvation, ethics, and the nature of God's redemptive plan.

- **Liturgical Practices and Eschatological Hope**

The Apocrypha's influence on liturgical practices is evident in traditions that include these texts in their worship. Certain prayers, hymns, and readings drawn from the Apocrypha contribute to liturgical expressions of eschatological hope and anticipation. The inclusion of passages that depict the resurrection of the righteous and the triumph of God's justice becomes a source of inspiration for believers as they engage in worship that looks forward to the fulfillment of eschatological promises.

In liturgical settings, eschatological themes from the Apocrypha are often woven into seasonal celebrations, emphasizing the Christian belief in the ultimate consummation of God's kingdom. The impact of these liturgical practices extends beyond theological reflections to shape the spiritual consciousness of believers, fostering a sense of hope and expectancy regarding the end times.

- **Popular Understanding of the End Times**

The Apocrypha's influence on Christian end-times beliefs is not limited to theological and liturgical contexts; it also permeates popular understandings of the end times. Narratives from the Apocrypha, such as the stories of courageous figures like Judith and the martyrs in Maccabees, become part of the collective Christian consciousness. These stories contribute to the popular imagery and symbolism associated with eschatological expectations.

Moreover, the apocalyptic visions and cosmic themes found in the Apocrypha resonate with popular interpretations of biblical prophecies and apocalyptic literature. The impact of these themes on popular eschatological beliefs is evident in various expressions of Christian culture, including literature, art, and media.

The Apocrypha, despite its varying status among different Christian denominations, continues to shape the imaginative landscape of Christian end-times beliefs.

Chapter Twenty Three

Apocrypha and Ethics

Moral and Ethical Teachings

The Apocrypha, a collection of texts that exists on the periphery of canonical Scripture for many, holds within its pages a wealth of moral and ethical teachings that resonate with the complexities of human existence. These teachings, often embedded in narratives, wisdom literature, and reflections on righteous living, contribute to the ethical framework within the Christian tradition.

One prominent example of moral teachings within the Apocrypha is found in the Book of Sirach

(Ecclesiasticus). This wisdom literature, attributed to Jesus, the son of Sirach, imparts practical guidance on various aspects of life. Sirach addresses topics ranging from familial relationships and social interactions to work ethics and personal conduct. The ethical teachings in Sirach reflect a commitment to virtue, justice, and integrity, providing a roadmap for navigating the moral challenges of daily life.

The Wisdom of Solomon, another book within the Apocrypha, explores ethical dimensions through reflections on divine wisdom. The ethical teachings within this text emphasize the alignment of human conduct with divine wisdom, promoting virtues such as humility, prudence, and righteousness. These teachings contribute to the ethical formation of individuals within the Christian tradition, guiding them towards a life characterized by moral uprightness and adherence to divine principles.

Virtues and Vices

Within the Apocrypha, a nuanced exploration of virtues and vices emerges, offering insights into the complexities of human character and the ethical choices individuals face. Virtues, understood as moral excellence and righteous qualities, are extolled as guides for virtuous living, while vices, representing moral failings and destructive behaviors, are presented as pitfalls to be avoided.

The Book of Tobit, for instance, illustrates the virtues of compassion, faithfulness, and piety. The central characters, Tobit and Tobias, exemplify these virtues in their actions and decisions. Tobit's commitment to charitable deeds, even in the face of adversity, highlights the ethical importance of compassion towards others. Tobias, guided by the angel Raphael, embodies faithfulness and piety as he navigates challenges and remains steadfast in his trust in God.

Conversely, the exploration of vices is evident in narratives such as the stories of Judith and Susanna. The portrayal of Holofernes in the Book of Judith represents the vices of arrogance, cruelty, and moral corruption. The narrative serves as a cautionary tale, illustrating the consequences of succumbing to destructive vices and the importance of resisting ethical compromise.

Ethical Dilemmas Explored

The Apocrypha delves into ethical dilemmas that confront individuals in various contexts, presenting nuanced narratives that invite reflection on the complexities of moral decision-making. These dilemmas, often woven into the fabric of captivating stories, provide readers with a lens through which to examine the ethical challenges inherent in the human experience.

In the Second Book of Maccabees, the narrative of the Maccabean martyrs unfolds as a poignant exploration of ethical dilemmas in the face of persecution. The martyrs, confronted with the choice between renouncing their faith and facing brutal consequences, grapple with profound ethical questions. The ethical dilemma of whether to compromise one's beliefs under duress or to stand firm in faith becomes a central theme, prompting readers to consider the cost of ethical decisions in the crucible of adversity.

The Book of Esther, while not universally included in the Apocrypha, presents another narrative rich in ethical dilemmas. Esther, a Jewish queen in the Persian court, faces the ethical challenge of revealing her identity and intervening on behalf of her people, risking her own safety. The narrative explores themes of courage, moral responsibility, and the ethical imperative to act in the face of injustice.

Chapter Twenty Four

Apocrypha in Liturgical Practices

Use in Worship

The Apocrypha, though debated in its canonicity, has found a significant place in liturgical practices within certain Christian traditions. The use of these texts in worship settings serves to enrich the tapestry of religious expression, offering a diverse range of narratives, prayers, and wisdom literature that contribute to the spiritual journey of believers.

In liturgical worship, passages from the Apocrypha are often incorporated into readings, psalms, and hymns. The Book of Tobit, for example, provides a poignant narrative of faith, trust in God's providence, and the importance of acts of charity. These themes resonate in liturgical settings where believers seek to draw inspiration for their own faith journeys. The ethical teachings found in Sirach become a source of reflection during worship, guiding individuals in their pursuit of moral and virtuous living.

Certain prayers and canticles from the Apocrypha, such as the Song of the Three Young Men in the fiery furnace from the Book of Daniel, find a place in liturgical worship. These poetic expressions of praise and trust in God's deliverance become integral components of worship experiences, allowing congregations to engage with the rich imagery and theological reflections present in the Apocrypha.

Festivals and Commemorations

The Apocrypha plays a distinctive role in festivals and commemorations within Christian traditions. Certain books, like the Wisdom of Solomon, contribute to theological reflections during feasts that celebrate wisdom and knowledge. Wisdom literature from the Apocrypha becomes a focal point during these celebrations, guiding believers to contemplate the divine source of wisdom and its relevance in their lives.

The festival of Hanukkah, rooted in the historical accounts found in the Apocryphal books of 1 and 2

Maccabees, commemorates the rededication of the Temple in Jerusalem. Readings from these books, particularly the accounts of the Maccabean revolt and the miracle of the oil, become central to Hanukkah observances. The Apocrypha thus informs the liturgical calendar, contributing narratives that connect believers with historical events and the enduring faith of those who resisted religious persecution.

Liturgical Readings

Liturgical readings from the Apocrypha vary across Christian denominations, reflecting the diverse approaches to these texts. In the Eastern Orthodox Church, for instance, the inclusion of certain Apocryphal books is more pronounced in liturgical readings compared to some Protestant traditions. Wisdom literature, such as that found in the Book of Wisdom, becomes a source of contemplation during specific liturgical seasons.

The Book of Judith, despite its varying canonicity, finds a place in liturgical readings during some Christian festivals. The narrative of Judith's bravery and her role in delivering her people from the Assyrian threat becomes a focal point for reflection on courage, trust in God, and the divine intervention in times of crisis.

Liturgical readings from the Apocrypha also extend to the celebration of saints. The stories of heroic figures like the Maccabean martyrs and the virtuous deeds of Tobit and Judith provide narratives that resonate with themes of faith, sacrifice, and righteousness. These readings become occasions for believers to draw inspiration from the lives of

these biblical characters, seeking

to emulate their virtues in their

own spiritual journeys.

Chapter Twenty Five

Apocrypha's Contribution to Christian Spirituality

Contemplative Practices

The Apocrypha, often regarded as a treasure trove of spiritual insights, significantly contributes to contemplative practices within Christian spirituality. Contemplation, a form of prayerful reflection and meditation, finds resonance in the rich narratives, wisdom literature, and ethical teachings embedded in the Apocrypha. Believers engaging in contemplative practices draw inspiration from the diverse stories and profound reflections found in these texts, cultivating a deeper connection with the divine.

The Book of Ecclesiasticus, or Sirach, emerges as a contemplative guide within the Apocrypha. Its wisdom literature provides practical reflections on virtuous living, guiding individuals in their contemplation on ethical choices and moral discernment. Contemplatives often turn to passages in Sirach to ponder the complexities of human relationships, the pursuit of wisdom, and the alignment of one's life with divine principles.

Contemplation within the Apocrypha extends to narratives like the Book of Tobit. The story of Tobit's unwavering faith, guided by the angel Raphael, becomes a focal point for contemplatives seeking to deepen their trust in divine providence. Through reflective engagement with Tobit's journey, individuals immerse themselves in contemplative practices that foster a profound reliance on God's guidance amid life's challenges.

Devotional Insights

The Apocrypha serves as a wellspring of devotional insights, offering believers a reservoir of inspiration for their spiritual journeys. Devotional practices, rooted in prayer, reflection, and a deepening relationship with the divine, find a rich source of material within the Apocrypha. From the heartfelt prayers of Tobit to the poetic reflections in the Wisdom of Solomon, these texts become guides for devotional engagement.

The Prayer of Azariah and the Song of the Three Young Men, found within the Book of Daniel, exemplify devotional expressions within the Apocrypha. These poetic prayers, uttered in the fiery furnace, reflect not only the courage of the three young men but also their deep trust in God's deliverance. Devotees draw upon these prayers as models for expressing trust, gratitude, and reliance on God in their own devotional practices.

Devotional insights within the Apocrypha extend to the Wisdom of Solomon, where profound reflections on divine wisdom become a source of contemplation and devotion. Believers engage with the poetic language and theological depth present in this text, using it as a guide for nurturing a heart inclined towards divine understanding and wisdom.

Spiritual Formation

The Apocrypha plays a vital role in the spiritual formation of individuals and communities within the Christian tradition. Spiritual formation, the process of being shaped and molded in one's spiritual journey, is enriched by the diverse themes and perspectives found in the Apocrypha. From narratives of faith and resilience to ethical teachings that guide moral character, these texts contribute to the holistic development of spiritual lives.

The stories of Judith and Esther, both of whom exhibited courage and conviction in critical moments, become integral to spiritual formation. Believers draw lessons on faithfulness, discernment, and the courage to act in the face of adversity. The transformative power of these narratives inspires individuals in their own spiritual journeys, fostering a resilient and faithful disposition.

Ethical teachings within the Apocrypha, exemplified in the wisdom literature of Sirach and Wisdom of Solomon, contribute to the moral and spiritual development of believers. As individuals engage with these texts in study and reflection, the ethical guidance embedded in the Apocrypha becomes a shaping force in their character formation, guiding them towards a life marked by virtue and righteousness.

PART VI: Comparative Analysis and Interfaith Dialogues

Chapter 26: Apocrypha in Comparative Religious Studies

Shared Themes across Faiths

In the expansive tapestry of religious traditions, the Apocrypha stands as a fascinating intersection where shared themes emerge across various faiths. While these texts hold distinct significance within Christian traditions, explorations in comparative religious studies reveal common threads that connect the Apocrypha to broader spiritual conversations. Themes such as wisdom, virtue, and the human experience resonate across faith boundaries, creating points of connection that invite interfaith exploration.

The Wisdom of Solomon, for instance, provides profound reflections on divine wisdom and its transformative power. In comparative studies, parallels can be drawn to wisdom literature in other religious traditions, such as the wisdom teachings found in Hindu scriptures or the philosophical insights in Islamic literature. The shared pursuit of wisdom as a guiding principle for ethical living becomes a bridge that fosters dialogue and understanding between diverse faith communities.

Narratives of resilience and faith, as exemplified in the stories of Tobit, Judith, and Esther, echo themes found in other religious texts. The universal human experiences of courage in the face of adversity, the triumph of good over evil, and the unwavering commitment to one's faith become touchpoints for interfaith dialogue. Exploring these shared narratives opens avenues for understanding the human condition from a broader, collective perspective.

Divergence in Interpretations

Despite shared themes, the Apocrypha also reveals divergence in interpretations across various religious traditions. Different faith communities bring their unique lenses and theological frameworks to these texts, shaping how they are understood and valued within each tradition. The Book of Tobit, for instance, may be regarded differently in a Christian context than in a Jewish or Islamic framework, leading to nuanced interpretations that reflect the theological distinctives of each faith.

The divergent interpretations of the Apocrypha are not only influenced by theological considerations but also by historical and cultural contexts. The story of Judith, celebrated for her bravery in Jewish and Christian traditions, may be viewed through distinct cultural lenses that shape its significance in different religious communities. Comparative religious studies delve into these nuances, unpacking how historical, cultural, and theological factors contribute to the varied interpretations of Apocryphal texts.

Examining the divergences in interpretations also reveals the richness of religious diversity. Rather than viewing differences as obstacles, comparative studies celebrate the multiplicity of perspectives and the ways in which religious communities find meaning and significance in the same texts. The Apocrypha, as a shared yet diverse reservoir of spiritual insights, becomes a platform for fostering respect and appreciation for the richness of global religious traditions.

Interfaith Dialogues

The Apocrypha, with its shared themes and divergent interpretations, becomes a valuable catalyst for interfaith dialogues. Interfaith dialogue involves a respectful exchange of beliefs, values, and perspectives between individuals of different religious traditions. The Apocrypha, acting as a common ground, provides a starting point for such conversations, inviting participants to explore shared spiritual principles and engage in meaningful discussions about their unique interpretations.

Interfaith dialogues often center around the ethical teachings present in the Apocrypha. Shared values of compassion, justice, and virtuous living become focal points for discussions that transcend religious boundaries. Participants may find common ground in the ethical guidance offered by Sirach or the reflections on righteous living found in the Wisdom of Solomon. These dialogues contribute to a deeper understanding of the shared moral fabric that connects diverse religious communities.

Challenges and differences in interpretations also become fruitful avenues for interfaith engagement. Rather than avoiding the complexities, interfaith dialogues that include discussions on divergent interpretations of Apocryphal texts provide opportunities for learning and mutual understanding. Participants gain insights into the theological nuances that shape each tradition's understanding of these texts, fostering an atmosphere of respect and openness.

Chapter Twenty Seven

Apocrypha and Jewish

Traditions

Jewish Perspectives on Apocryphal

Writings

Within the vast and intricate landscape of Jewish traditions, the Apocrypha stands as a collection of writings that elicit diverse perspectives, reflective of the rich tapestry of Jewish thought. Jewish scholars and communities engage with these writings with a nuanced approach, acknowledging their historical context and distinctiveness from the canonical Scriptures. The

Wisdom of Solomon and Sirach, for example, are often valued for their ethical teachings and reflections on divine wisdom. While not considered part of the Hebrew Bible, these texts have found a place within Jewish literature, prompting discussions on their significance and relevance.

Jewish perspectives on the Apocrypha are shaped by a deep commitment to preserving the authenticity of the Hebrew Scriptures. The recognition of a distinct canon, commonly referred to as the Tanakh, influences how Jewish communities view Apocryphal writings. While some communities may explore these texts in historical and cultural contexts, others may approach them with caution, emphasizing the sanctity of the established canon. This nuanced engagement contributes to the ongoing dialogue within Jewish traditions about the scope and boundaries of sacred texts, inviting a continuous exploration of the intricate intersections between the canonical and the Apocryphal.

Historical Connections

The Apocrypha shares historical connections with Jewish traditions that extend beyond its canonical status. Texts like 1 and 2 Maccabees, recounting the historical events surrounding the Maccabean Revolt, provide invaluable insights into a pivotal period in Jewish history. These writings offer narratives of courage, resilience, and devotion to God that resonate with Jewish communities, illustrating the profound interplay between historical events and religious identity.

The Book of Judith, while not included in the Hebrew Bible, is celebrated for its depiction of a courageous Jewish heroine. Judith's daring act to save her people from the Assyrian general Holofernes is commemorated in Jewish cultural expressions, including art and literature. The historical connections forged through these narratives contribute to a shared sense of identity and remembrance within Jewish traditions, acknowledging the enduring impact of events captured in Apocryphal writings on the collective memory of the Jewish people.

The exploration of historical connections between the Apocrypha and Jewish traditions goes beyond mere chronicles; it becomes a dynamic engagement with the roots of identity and the shaping forces that have influenced the development of Jewish communities over centuries. The Apocrypha, in this context, acts as a reservoir of historical narratives that inform the understanding of the Jewish past and its enduring impact on contemporary Jewish identity.

Shared Ethical Values

Ethical values embedded in the Apocrypha find a deep resonance in Jewish traditions, offering a source of shared wisdom and moral reflection. The ethical teachings present in Sirach, also known as Ecclesiasticus, provide practical guidance on virtuous living. Jewish communities appreciate the emphasis on wisdom, filial piety, and the pursuit of righteousness found in this text. The Wisdom of Solomon similarly contributes to discussions on ethical conduct, exploring themes of justice, humility, and the fear of God.

Jewish ethical values intersect with those portrayed in the Apocrypha, fostering a shared commitment to principles that guide personal and communal life. The story of Tobit, with its emphasis on acts of kindness and compassion, resonates with Jewish teachings on gemilut chasadim, acts of loving-kindness. The shared ethical fabric between these Apocryphal writings and Jewish traditions becomes a bridge that connects diverse expressions of faith, reinforcing the common pursuit of moral integrity that is foundational to both Jewish and Apocryphal ethical teachings.

This intersection of ethical values becomes a point of convergence, fostering a deeper understanding of the moral principles that shape the lives of individuals and communities. It transcends the boundaries of scriptural canonicity, creating a shared space for ethical reflection and moral guidance that is both rooted in tradition and open to dynamic interpretations. The Apocrypha, in its ethical dimensions, contributes to an ongoing conversation within Jewish traditions about the timeless principles that guide human conduct.

Chapter Twenty Eight

Apocrypha and Islamic Perspectives

Common Narratives and Characters

In the intricate tapestry of religious traditions, the Apocrypha, a collection of writings often situated at the periphery of Christian canonicity, unexpectedly finds threads woven into the fabric of Islamic perspectives. The intersection between the Apocrypha and Islamic thought reveals surprising parallels in narratives and characters that bridge the gap between these two Abrahamic faiths. Commonalities emerge not only in the

256

retelling of certain historical events but also in the shared reverence for figures whose stories traverse the boundaries of canonical distinctions.

Islamic traditions exhibit an intriguing familiarity with characters like Adam, Noah, and Abraham, figures whose narratives extend beyond the canonical boundaries of the Qur'an and resonate with stories found in the Apocrypha. The accounts of these patriarchal figures, while presented in distinct theological frameworks, evoke a sense of shared heritage. Adam's creation, Noah's ark, and Abraham's journey become points of convergence, illustrating the interconnectedness of narratives that transcend religious labels. The Apocrypha, often viewed as a reservoir of supplementary stories, contributes to a broader understanding of shared sacred history between Christianity and Islam.

Influence on Islamic Thought

The influence of the Apocrypha on Islamic thought extends beyond shared narratives to nuanced theological reflections. While the Qur'an stands as the primary source of revelation in Islam, the Apocrypha, with its historical and ethical dimensions, has contributed to the diverse tapestry of Islamic intellectual discourse. Themes such as divine wisdom, prophetic visions, and ethical teachings found in texts like the Wisdom of Solomon and Sirach resonate with Islamic perspectives on the nature of God, the role of prophets, and the ethical principles guiding human conduct.

The Apocrypha's impact on Islamic thought is evident in the echoes of its themes within Sufi mysticism. The emphasis on divine love, spiritual insight, and the pursuit of wisdom, often found in Apocryphal writings, aligns with the mystical dimensions of Islam. Sufi poets and philosophers draw inspiration from the broader spiritual landscape represented by the Apocrypha, enriching Islamic spirituality with diverse perspectives on the mystical journey and the transcendent nature of God.

Areas of Disagreement

However, the relationship between the Apocrypha and Islamic perspectives is not devoid of complexities. Areas of disagreement arise, particularly concerning doctrinal and historical differences. The Apocrypha's exploration of certain theological themes, such as the nature of God and the divine-human relationship, may diverge from Islamic theological positions, leading to theological disparities. Islamic scholars, guided by the Qur'an and Hadith, may approach Apocryphal writings with caution, discerning between shared narratives and theological nuances.

The differing perspectives on figures like Jesus, portrayed in unique ways within the Apocrypha, can also contribute to theological divergence. While Islamic traditions honor Jesus as a prophet, the Apocrypha's portrayal of Jesus in various roles, including mystical teacher and revealer of hidden knowledge, may present theological challenges within an Islamic framework. These areas of disagreement underscore the importance of recognizing the distinct theological lenses through which each faith interprets shared narratives.

Chapter 29:

Apocrypha and Eastern Christian Traditions

Byzantine and Oriental Orthodox Views

Within the Byzantine and Oriental Orthodox traditions, the Apocrypha holds a distinct place, serving as a source of spiritual nourishment and theological reflection. Unlike some Western Christian denominations, these Eastern traditions have maintained a broader acceptance of the Apocryphal books, considering them valuable for understanding the historical and theological context of the Christian faith. The Byzantine Orthodox Church, with its historical roots in the Eastern Roman Empire, holds a deep appreciation for the Apocrypha as part of the broader Christian literary heritage. Similarly, the Oriental Orthodox Churches, encompassing traditions such as the Coptic, Ethiopian, and Armenian, embrace the Apocrypha as integral to their religious and cultural identity.

Liturgical Practices

Liturgical practices within Eastern Christian traditions reflect the reverence accorded to the Apocrypha. These ancient communities engage in liturgical readings that incorporate passages from these texts, enriching the worship experience with narratives not found in the standard Western canon. The Wisdom of Solomon and Sirach, for example, resonate within the liturgical hymns and prayers, offering profound insights into the pursuit of divine wisdom and ethical living. The Apocrypha becomes a dynamic component of Eastern Christian worship, fostering a deeper connection with the spiritual heritage passed down through generations.

Cultural Adaptations

The Apocrypha's influence extends beyond the sanctuary, permeating the cultural expressions of Eastern Christian communities. In Byzantine iconography, scenes from Apocryphal narratives find vivid depiction, contributing to the visual narrative of Christian salvation history. The stories of Judith's courage, Tobit's piety, and the angelic revelations in the Book of Enoch become not only theological reflections but also cultural touchstones that shape the artistic and literary expressions of Byzantine and Oriental Orthodox societies.

Cultural adaptations also manifest in the vibrant traditions of Eastern Christian storytelling. The Apocrypha's narratives, with their vivid characters and moral teachings, become foundational elements in the oral traditions of these communities. From the Ethiopian Highlands to the monastic enclaves of Mount Athos, the Apocrypha's tales echo through the ages, passed down from one generation to the next. These cultural adaptations not only preserve the richness of the Apocryphal narratives but also contribute to the distinctive identity of Eastern Christian traditions.

Chapter Thirty

Apocrypha and Global Christian Traditions

Adoption and Reception

The Apocrypha, often referred to as the hidden or concealed writings, has journeyed through time, transcending geographical boundaries, and finding a home within the diverse tapestry of global Christian traditions. Its adoption and reception among various Christian denominations worldwide have created a mosaic of theological perspectives and cultural expressions that enrich the shared heritage of the faith.

266

As believers from different corners of the globe engage with these texts, the Apocrypha becomes a bridge connecting believers across continents, fostering a global Christian dialogue that resonates with the unity in diversity inherent in Christianity.

The adoption of the Apocrypha within global Christian traditions is a testament to the dynamic nature of the Christian faith. While some denominations include these texts as an integral part of their biblical canon, others acknowledge them as valuable historical and theological resources without considering them on par with the canonical Scriptures. In the Eastern Orthodox Churches, the Apocrypha has found a longstanding place within the biblical canon, contributing to liturgical practices and theological discourse. The Ethiopian Orthodox

Tewahedo Church, with its rich cultural heritage, embraces the Apocrypha not only as sacred texts but also as foundational elements shaping its distinctive Christian identity.

Ecumenical Implications

The Apocrypha holds significant ecumenical implications, serving as a point of convergence and divergence among Christian traditions. While differences in canonization exist, the shared narratives and theological themes present in the Apocrypha create a common ground for dialogue and understanding. The ecumenical movement, which seeks to promote unity among diverse Christian traditions, finds both challenges and opportunities in the varying attitudes towards the Apocrypha.

In ecumenical dialogues, the Apocrypha becomes a locus for theological discussions, inviting believers to explore the richness of their shared heritage and the divergences that have shaped their distinct theological identities. Recognizing the varied reception of the Apocrypha among Christians fosters a spirit of humility and mutual respect, acknowledging the diversity that exists within the global Christian family. The ecumenical implications extend beyond theological considerations to encompass shared ethical values, spiritual practices, and the collective mission of Christians in addressing contemporary global challenges.

Contemporary Relevance

In the midst of the diverse currents of contemporary Christianity, the Apocrypha maintains its relevance, offering insights that resonate with the challenges and aspirations of believers worldwide. The narratives of Tobit's unwavering faith, Judith's courage, and the apocalyptic visions in the Book of Enoch speak to the human condition, transcending cultural and geographical boundaries. The Apocrypha becomes a source of inspiration for believers navigating the complexities of the modern world, providing them with timeless wisdom and moral guidance.

Contemporary Christian worship and spiritual practices often draw from the Apocrypha, incorporating its themes into liturgical hymns, prayers, and artistic expressions.

The wisdom literature found in Sirach and Wisdom of Solomon, for example, continues to shape Christian ethical reflections and provide a moral compass for believers seeking to live out their faith in a rapidly changing world. The Apocrypha's relevance extends to the intersection of faith and culture, influencing the way believers engage with issues such as social justice, environmental stewardship, and the pursuit of peace.

Moreover, the Apocrypha's contemporary relevance is evident in its impact on theological education and scholarship. The exploration of these texts opens avenues for deeper theological reflection, encouraging believers to engage critically with their faith and fostering a robust understanding of the Christian tradition. The Apocrypha invites Christians to wrestle with theological questions, grapple with the complexities

of biblical interpretation, and embrace a faith that is both

ancient and ever new.

PART VII: Textual Criticism

and Scholarship

Chapter Thirty One

Textual History of the Apocrypha

Manuscript Discoveries

The journey of the Apocrypha through the annals of history is intricately woven into the fabric of manuscript discoveries. The quest to uncover and preserve these ancient texts has been a voyage marked by both serendipity and scholarly rigor. The manuscripts containing the Apocrypha have emerged from diverse corners of the world, revealing a fascinating narrative of preservation and rediscovery.

One of the pivotal moments in the textual history of the Apocrypha was the discovery of the Codex Sinaiticus in the mid-19th century. This ancient manuscript, dating back to the 4th century, contained a remarkable collection of biblical texts, including several books of the Apocrypha. Unearthed at the Monastery of St. Catherine on Mount Sinai, this codex provided scholars with invaluable insights into the textual traditions of the Apocrypha. Similarly, the Codex Alexandrinus, discovered in the 17th century, illuminated the transmission of these texts within the Byzantine tradition.

Beyond these renowned manuscripts, numerous fragments and scrolls have been unearthed in archaeological excavations. The Dead Sea Scrolls, a treasure trove found in the caves of Qumran, included fragments of Apocryphal books such as Tobit and Sirach. These discoveries shed light on the diverse textual traditions and the regional variations that characterized the transmission of the Apocrypha.

Transmission and Preservation

The transmission of the Apocrypha across centuries is a testament to the meticulous efforts of scribes, scholars, and communities dedicated to preserving these sacred writings. The Apocrypha's journey through time involved the laborious process of copying manuscripts by hand, a task undertaken with reverence and precision to ensure the faithful transmission of the sacred texts.

The transmission of the Apocrypha faced unique challenges, given its status as non-canonical in some Christian traditions. While certain manuscripts included the Apocrypha alongside the canonical books, others separated them or omitted certain texts altogether. The decisions made by scribes and communities during the transmission process reflected theological considerations, regional practices, and the evolving understanding of the Apocrypha's place within the Christian canon.

Preservation efforts extended beyond the scriptoria of monasteries to the hearts of communities that revered the Apocrypha. Liturgical practices, such as the reading of Tobit during the Festival of Purim, contributed to the preservation of these texts within the fabric of communal worship. The Apocrypha became not only a written record but a living tradition, passed down from generation to generation through the rhythms of Christian worship and devotion.

Textual Variants

The textual history of the Apocrypha is marked by a rich tapestry of variants, reflecting the diverse traditions and interpretations that flourished across different Christian communities. Textual variants encompass not only differences in wording but also variations in the inclusion or omission of specific passages, adding layers of complexity to the study of the Apocrypha.

One of the notable instances of textual variation is found in the Book of Esther, where the Greek version includes additional verses not present in the Hebrew Masoretic Text. This expansion, known as the "Additions to Esther," provides insights into the dynamic nature of biblical texts and the fluidity of their transmission. Similarly, the Book of Daniel in the Apocrypha contains additions, including the Prayer of Azariah and the Song of the Three Jews, which are absent from the Hebrew Bible.

The study of textual variants in the Apocrypha requires a nuanced approach, acknowledging the diverse manuscript traditions and the theological motivations that shaped these variations. Scholars engage in meticulous textual criticism, comparing manuscripts and versions to reconstruct the earliest possible form of the texts. The existence of textual variants invites reflection on the fluidity of the biblical text and the interpretative

flexibility within Christian communities.

Chapter Thirty Two

Scholarly Debates on

Apocryphal Authenticity

Academic Perspectives

The scholarly exploration of the Apocrypha has been a terrain marked by diverse perspectives, each seeking to unravel the authenticity and significance of these enigmatic texts. Academic engagement with the Apocrypha involves a multifaceted approach, where historians, theologians, and textual critics converge in a dialogue that stretches across centuries. The academic perspectives on the Apocrypha reflect a spectrum of views, from those that champion its historical value to others that scrutinize its theological implications.

Historical scholars delve into the Apocrypha with a keen eye on uncovering the historical contexts in which these texts emerged. They scrutinize the cultural milieu, linguistic nuances, and socio-political landscapes that shaped the narratives. For instance, the Books of Maccabees provide invaluable historical insights into the Hellenistic period and the struggles of the Jewish people for religious autonomy. By examining these texts alongside other historical sources, scholars weave together a tapestry that enhances our understanding of the times in which the Apocrypha unfolded.

Theological perspectives within academia bring forth a rich tapestry of discussions on the nature of God, divine revelation, and the intersection of human and divine. The Apocrypha, with its diverse theological themes, becomes a reservoir for exploring questions of faith, morality, and the divine-human relationship. Theological debates often revolve around the doctrinal implications of specific Apocryphal teachings, and scholars engage in rigorous discussions on how these texts contribute to the broader theological landscape of Christianity.

Historical Criticism

Historical criticism emerges as a key methodology employed by scholars in their quest to discern the authenticity of Apocryphal texts. This approach involves a meticulous examination of the historical context, authorship, and transmission of biblical writings. Within the realm of Apocrypha, historical criticism seeks to unveil the origins of these texts, identifying the cultural, religious, and political forces that shaped their composition.

The question of authorship becomes a focal point for historical critics, who carefully analyze the linguistic style, cultural references, and ideological underpinnings of each book. For instance, the Book of Wisdom, attributed to Solomon, undergoes scrutiny to assess its alignment with the wisdom literature of the ancient Near East. Similarly, historical critics delve into the circumstances surrounding the writing of Tobit or the historical events depicted in Judith.

Transmission history also falls under the purview of historical criticism, as scholars trace the journey of Apocryphal texts from their original composition to the manuscript discoveries of later centuries. The study of textual variants, manuscript traditions, and the influence of different cultural and religious communities becomes integral to historical criticism. Through these investigations, scholars strive to reconstruct the earliest form of the Apocrypha and discern the layers of interpretation added over time.

Theological Implications

Theological implications of the Apocrypha form a nexus where scholars grapple with questions of canonization, inspiration, and the authority of sacred texts. The diversity of theological themes within the Apocrypha raises profound questions about their relationship with the canonical books and their role in shaping Christian doctrine.

One theological consideration revolves around the process of canonization – the inclusion or exclusion of texts within the biblical canon. Scholars explore the criteria employed by different Christian traditions in recognizing certain books as canonical while relegating others, like the Apocrypha, to a secondary status. Theological discussions weigh the factors of inspiration, orthodoxy, and communal reception in the formation of the biblical canon.

The Apocrypha's theological implications extend to its influence on Christian thought and practice. Texts such as Tobit and Sirach offer ethical teachings and practical wisdom that have resonated with believers throughout history. The theological richness of these writings invites reflection on the broader theological landscape of Christianity and the dynamic interplay between canonical and non-canonical texts.

Chapter Thirty Three

Translation Challenges and Solutions

Translating Lost Books

The task of translating the lost books of the Bible, collectively known as the Apocrypha, is a journey through linguistic landscapes and cultural nuances, fraught with both challenges and opportunities. As translators embark on the daunting mission of rendering ancient texts into contemporary languages, they confront the inherent difficulties tied to the preservation of meaning, context, and the delicate intricacies of the original writings.

One significant challenge in translating the lost books lies in the gaps of understanding that have naturally accumulated over centuries. The Apocrypha, being a collection of texts with origins in diverse regions and cultures, presents linguistic complexities that arise from archaic expressions, idiomatic usages, and linguistic subtleties lost to time. Navigating through these linguistic time capsules requires not only linguistic expertise but also a deep understanding of the cultural contexts in which these texts emerged.

The very nature of the lost books, having been excluded from certain historical canons, adds another layer of complexity. Translators face the task of not merely converting words from one language to another but also of bridging the gap between the cultural and theological realms embedded within the texts. The challenge is not just to render the words in a comprehensible form but to capture the essence and intended meaning of the original, often elusive in the shadows of history.

Linguistic Nuances

Linguistic nuances pose a formidable challenge in the translation of the Apocrypha. The linguistic tapestry of these ancient texts includes a rich variety of languages such as Hebrew, Aramaic, and Greek. Each language carries its own set of nuances, idioms, and linguistic idiosyncrasies, demanding a nuanced approach in translation to convey the depth and subtlety of the original messages.

The challenge intensifies when dealing with idiomatic expressions that may lack direct equivalents in modern languages. Translators face the delicate task of not only capturing the literal meaning but also preserving the cultural connotations and metaphorical layers embedded in these expressions. This demands a high degree of linguistic finesse and cultural sensitivity to ensure that the translated words resonate with the same depth and impact as their ancient counterparts.

The choice of words itself becomes a crucial aspect in navigating linguistic nuances. Some words in the Apocrypha may have evolved in meaning or fallen out of common usage, necessitating careful consideration in selecting words that accurately convey the intended sense without losing the historical and theological dimensions. Striking a balance between linguistic accuracy and accessibility becomes a delicate art, demanding both scholarly acumen and a profound respect for the integrity of the original texts.

Cultural Considerations

Translation of the Apocrypha extends beyond linguistic challenges to encompass the broader realm of cultural considerations. The cultural context in which these texts originated significantly shapes their meanings, and translators must grapple with the task of transplanting these meanings into the cultural landscape of contemporary readers.

Cultural considerations encompass not only linguistic elements but also the broader socio-religious contexts in which the Apocrypha emerged. Each book carries the imprint of its cultural milieu, reflecting the beliefs, practices, and historical circumstances of its time. Translators face the challenge of not only conveying the literal meanings of words but also capturing the cultural ethos that underlies the narratives and teachings.

Moreover, the cultural distance between the ancient world and the present poses challenges in ensuring that the translated texts remain relevant and relatable to modern readers. The translator becomes a cultural mediator, striving to make the voices of the past resonate with the sensibilities of the present without compromising the authenticity of the original messages.

Chapter Thirty Four

Modern Scholarly

Contributions

Recent Research and Discoveries

In the ever-evolving landscape of biblical scholarship, the study of the Apocrypha has witnessed a resurgence of interest, propelled by recent research initiatives and groundbreaking discoveries. Modern scholars, armed with advanced tools of archaeology, linguistics, and textual analysis, have delved into the depths of historical archives and ancient manuscripts, unearthing hidden treasures that enrich our understanding of the lost books of the Bible.

Recent excavations and archaeological findings have unearthed fragments and scrolls that shed new light on the Apocrypha's textual history. The discovery of previously unknown manuscripts has provided scholars with fresh material for analysis, offering glimpses into variant readings, linguistic nuances, and contextual details that were previously obscured. These discoveries not only expand the corpus of Apocryphal texts but also fuel scholarly debates on authenticity, transmission, and the interconnectedness of ancient literary traditions.

Scholarly Publications

The realm of Apocryphal studies has witnessed a proliferation of scholarly publications, reflecting a vibrant academic discourse that spans a spectrum of disciplines. The academic community, driven by a commitment to rigorous research and intellectual inquiry, has produced a plethora of monographs, articles, and critical editions dedicated to unraveling the mysteries of the Apocrypha.

These scholarly publications delve into diverse aspects of Apocryphal studies, ranging from textual criticism and historical contextualization to theological reflections and comparative analyses. Researchers explore the linguistic nuances of Apocryphal texts, offering insights into translation challenges and textual variants.

Historical-critical approaches unravel the socio-political and religious contexts in which these texts emerged, providing a nuanced understanding of their significance in antiquity.

Advancements in Apocryphal Studies

Advancements in technology and interdisciplinary collaborations have propelled Apocryphal studies into new frontiers. Digital tools and databases have revolutionized the accessibility of ancient manuscripts, allowing scholars to engage with textual variants, conduct comparative analyses, and trace the evolution of Apocryphal traditions with unprecedented precision. This digital age has facilitated a democratization of knowledge, enabling researchers and enthusiasts alike to

explore the richness of the Apocrypha from diverse
vantage points.

Interdisciplinary collaborations have become a hallmark
of modern Apocryphal studies. Scholars from fields as
diverse as archaeology, linguistics, theology, and cultural
studies converge to enrich the discourse surrounding the
lost books of the Bible. This interdisciplinary approach
not only deepens our understanding of the Apocrypha
but also fosters a holistic appreciation of the multifaceted
dimensions embedded within these ancient texts.

Chapter Thirty Five

Future Directions in

Apocryphal Research

Emerging Trends

The landscape of Apocryphal research is poised on the cusp of transformative developments, driven by emerging trends that promise to shape the trajectory of scholarship in the coming years. One notable trend revolves around the integration of technological innovations into the study of the Apocrypha. As advancements in artificial intelligence, digital humanities, and computational linguistics gain momentum, scholars are exploring new methodologies to enhance the analysis and interpretation of Apocryphal texts. Computational tools enable the identification of linguistic patterns, textual variants, and intertextual relationships, opening avenues for a more nuanced understanding of the intricate tapestry woven by these ancient writings.

Another significant trend involves the increasing emphasis on interdisciplinary collaborations. Recognizing the multifaceted nature of Apocryphal literature, scholars from diverse fields such as anthropology, psychology, and comparative religion are joining forces to explore the broader cultural, social, and psychological dimensions embedded within these texts. This interdisciplinary approach not only enriches the contextualization of Apocryphal writings but also fosters a holistic understanding of their impact on diverse communities across time and space.

Collaborative Projects

The future of Apocryphal research is characterized by a spirit of collaboration, as scholars embark on joint ventures and collaborative projects that transcend institutional and geographical boundaries. Collaborations between academic institutions, research centers, and religious organizations are becoming increasingly common, pooling resources and expertise to address complex questions surrounding the Apocrypha. Such collaborative endeavors facilitate the sharing of diverse perspectives, methodologies, and resources, fostering a more comprehensive and inclusive approach to Apocryphal studies.

One notable collaborative trend involves the creation of comprehensive databases and digital repositories dedicated to Apocryphal literature. These repositories serve as centralized hubs for scholars and enthusiasts, providing easy access to a wealth of manuscripts, translations, and critical editions. The collaborative digitization of ancient manuscripts ensures their preservation and widens accessibility, democratizing the study of the Apocrypha and inviting a global community to engage with these profound texts.

Areas for Further Exploration

The future of Apocryphal research beckons scholars to explore uncharted territories and delve into areas that have remained obscured by the mists of time. One such area for further exploration involves a more robust engagement with the reception history of the Apocrypha. Understanding how these texts have been received, interpreted, and incorporated into the theological fabric of various Christian denominations throughout history can provide valuable insights into their enduring significance.

Furthermore, scholars are called to explore the intersectionality of Apocryphal literature with issues of social justice, ethics, and environmental stewardship. Integrating the ethical teachings embedded within the

Apocrypha into contemporary discourse can inspire conversations on morality, compassion, and responsible living. The exploration of these themes resonates with the timeless relevance of the Apocrypha, transcending historical and cultural contexts to address pressing issues in our modern world.

PART VIII: Conclusion and

Reflections

Chapter Thirty Six

The Legacy of the Apocrypha

Enduring Impact

The legacy of the Apocrypha is a testament to the enduring impact of these ancient writings on the tapestry of Christian history and thought. As we delve into the rich layers of this literary heritage, it becomes evident that the Apocrypha, though often residing on the fringes of the canonical boundaries, has left an indelible mark on the development of Christian theology and spirituality. Its enduring impact is woven into the fabric of the Christian narrative, contributing to the diverse theological expressions that have shaped the identity of countless believers throughout the centuries.

The Apocrypha's enduring impact is particularly pronounced in its ability to offer alternative perspectives on familiar biblical narratives. Through stories of extraordinary courage, wisdom, and divine intervention, these texts provide readers with nuanced insights into the human experience and the divine-human relationship. The characters within the Apocrypha, often relegated to the periphery, step into the foreground, challenging readers to reconsider their roles and significance within the overarching biblical narrative. This alternative lens not only enriches the reader's understanding of the biblical world but also invites a deeper engagement with the complexities of faith and human existence.

Influence on Christian Thought

The influence of the Apocrypha on Christian thought is a multifaceted journey that traverses theological, ethical, and liturgical landscapes. Within the theological realm, the Apocrypha contributes to a broader understanding of foundational doctrines, such as the nature of God, divine providence, and eschatology. The theological insights embedded within these texts, while distinctive, complement the canonical scriptures, providing a holistic framework for grappling with the mysteries of faith. The Apocrypha's influence extends beyond doctrinal formulations, fostering a rich theological diversity that has contributed to the vibrant tapestry of Christian thought.

Ethically, the Apocrypha engages with the complexities of human virtue, vice, and moral decision-making. Characters grappling with ethical dilemmas, navigating issues of justice and righteousness, offer readers a nuanced exploration of the ethical dimensions of faith. The Apocrypha's ethical teachings, embedded within narratives and wisdom literature, serve as a moral compass, guiding believers in their quest for virtuous living and ethical discernment.

Liturgically, the Apocrypha's impact is evident in its incorporation into worship practices and religious festivals. While not universally accepted across Christian traditions, certain segments of the Apocrypha are included in liturgical readings, adding depth and variety to the worship experience. The Apocrypha's influence on liturgy extends beyond the confines of sacred texts to inspire hymns, prayers, and artistic expressions that resonate with the spiritual sensibilities of diverse Christian communities.

Relevance in the 21st Century

In the ever-evolving landscape of the 21st century, the Apocrypha continues to exert its relevance, offering profound insights that resonate with contemporary challenges and aspirations. Its relevance lies in its ability to speak to the complexities of the human condition, addressing existential questions, ethical quandaries, and the quest for spiritual meaning. The Apocrypha's narratives, though rooted in ancient contexts, bridge the temporal gap, inviting readers to find resonance between the struggles of biblical characters and the challenges of modern life.

Moreover, the Apocrypha's relevance extends to its potential for fostering interfaith dialogue and understanding. As global communities navigate a diverse tapestry of beliefs and practices, the Apocrypha serves as a point of intersection, offering shared narratives and ethical teachings that transcend religious boundaries. The exploration of common ground within the Apocrypha opens avenues for dialogue, fostering mutual respect and collaboration among individuals of different faith traditions.

Chapter Thirty Seven

Personal Reflections

Individual Perspectives

Within the pages of "The Complete 50 Lost Book Apocrypha," the journey of personal reflection embarks on a profound exploration of individual perspectives. Each reader encounters these ancient texts through a unique lens, shaped by personal experiences, cultural backgrounds, and spiritual predispositions. The Apocrypha, often considered the hidden treasure of biblical literature, invites readers to navigate its narratives, wisdom literature, and historical accounts with a sense of curiosity and openness. As individuals engage with these sacred writings, diverse perspectives emerge, contributing to the collective tapestry of spiritual understanding.

These individual perspectives encompass a spectrum of responses, ranging from intellectual curiosity to deep emotional resonance. Some readers may approach the Apocrypha as a historical artifact, unraveling the mysteries of ancient civilizations and their religious expressions. Others may find solace in the Apocrypha's wisdom literature, seeking guidance for navigating the complexities of life's ethical dilemmas. The Apocrypha's blend of narratives and teachings creates a space where diverse intellectual, emotional, and spiritual perspectives converge, fostering a rich tapestry of individual engagement.

Spiritual Journeys

As readers embark on spiritual journeys through the Apocrypha, they find themselves traversing landscapes of faith, doubt, and discovery. The narratives within these hidden books unfold as sacred maps, guiding individuals through the terrain of their own spiritual pilgrimages. The Apocrypha, with its enigmatic stories and profound reflections, becomes a companion on the journey of faith, providing moments of illumination, challenge, and reassurance.

For some, the spiritual journey within the Apocrypha is marked by encounters with the divine in unexpected places. The hidden gems of these texts reveal facets of the divine-human relationship that resonate with the complexities of contemporary spirituality. Characters grappling with faith in the face of adversity, seeking divine guidance in moments of despair, and navigating the intricate pathways of spiritual discernment become companions for readers navigating their own spiritual landscapes. The Apocrypha, far from being a mere historical artifact, unfolds as a living testament to the perennial quest for meaning and connection with the divine.

Transformative Encounters

At the heart of "The Complete 50 Lost Book Apocrypha" lies the potential for transformative encounters that transcend the boundaries of time and tradition. Readers may find themselves unexpectedly transformed as they delve into the stories of courageous women, visionary prophets, and ordinary individuals thrust into extraordinary circumstances. These encounters spark a process of self-discovery, inviting readers to reflect on their own lives, beliefs, and values in light of the timeless truths embedded within the Apocrypha.

The transformative power of these encounters is not confined to the intellectual realm; it extends to the emotional and moral dimensions of the human experience. The Apocrypha's narratives, which often illuminate the complexities of human virtue and vice, offer readers a mirror to examine their own ethical choices and moral convictions. In moments of reflection, readers may find themselves inspired to embody virtues demonstrated by the characters within these sacred texts or to confront vices that echo through the corridors of biblical history.

Chapter Thirty Eight

Closing Thoughts on Lost

Books

Acknowledging Diversity

As we draw the curtain on the exploration of "The Complete 50 Lost Book Apocrypha," it is imperative to acknowledge the richness of diversity encapsulated within these lost books. These writings, often hidden from the conventional canon, offer a kaleidoscope of perspectives, narratives, and theological reflections that underscore the vastness of the Christian tradition. The acknowledgment of diversity within the Apocrypha is an invitation to appreciate the multifaceted nature of Christian thought and spirituality.

Within these lost books, we encounter a diversity of literary genres, from historical narratives and wisdom literature to apocalyptic visions and pseudepigraphical writings. Each genre contributes distinctively to the theological tapestry, unveiling layers of meaning and insight. The diversity within the Apocrypha extends beyond literary forms; it encompasses theological nuances, ethical reflections, and cultural adaptations that resonate with the manifold expressions of Christian faith. The acknowledgment of this diversity invites readers to embrace the richness of their Christian heritage and engage with the broader spectrum of theological discourse embedded in these forgotten texts.

Unity in Christian Faith

Despite the acknowledgment of diversity, "The Complete 50 Lost Book Apocrypha" serves as a reminder of the profound unity that binds Christians across different traditions and denominations. While the canonization of biblical texts varies among Christian communities, the overarching narrative of redemption, divine love, and human reconciliation remains a unifying force. The lost books within the Apocrypha, in their diversity, contribute to this unity by affirming the shared values, beliefs, and foundational narratives that define Christian faith.

The Apocrypha's narratives, whether recounting historical events or presenting ethical teachings, converge on the central theme of God's redemptive plan for humanity. This unity in purpose and vision transcends denominational boundaries, inviting Christians to find common ground in their shared commitment to follow Christ and live out the teachings of love, justice, and compassion. The exploration of the Apocrypha serves as a poignant reminder that, despite theological diversity, Christians are bound together by a shared heritage and a collective journey toward a deeper understanding of God's unfolding plan.

The Ongoing Conversation

"The Complete 50 Lost Book Apocrypha" concludes not as a finality but as an invitation to an ongoing conversation. The exploration of these lost books does not mark the end of the Christian theological journey; instead, it propels believers into a continuous dialogue with their sacred texts and with one another. The Apocrypha, with its mysteries and revelations, opens a space for contemplation, inquiry, and interpretation, fostering a vibrant conversation within the Christian community.

This ongoing conversation embraces the questions that arise from the exploration of the Apocrypha—questions about the nature of God, the complexities of human existence, and the ethical imperatives of Christian living. It encourages believers to engage with their faith critically, recognizing that the Christian journey involves wrestling with theological concepts, navigating the complexities of scripture, and seeking deeper insights through communal discernment. The ongoing conversation is not confined to the realm of theology alone; it extends to the lived experiences of believers, inviting them to reflect on how the teachings within the Apocrypha shape their individual and communal Christian identities.

In conclusion, "The Complete 50 Lost Book Apocrypha" stands as both a testament to diversity and a beacon of unity within the Christian faith. As readers traverse the landscapes of forgotten narratives, wisdom literature, and apocalyptic visions, they are invited to acknowledge the richness of their Christian heritage, find unity in shared foundational narratives, and engage in an ongoing conversation that propels them toward a deeper understanding of God's redemptive plan. The lost books, though often hidden, continue to speak, challenge, and inspire, inviting believers into a transformative journey that transcends the confines of canonization and echoes

through the corridors of Christian history.

.

The Complete 50 Lost Book Apocrypha

Printed in Great Britain
by Amazon

9de2c767-90e8-4257-9971-c08f6495b314R01